W9-CMC-982

GET OUT OF YOUR OWN WAY GUIDE TO LIFE

10 STEPS TO SHIFT GEARS, DREAM BIG, DO IT NOW!

JUSTIN LOEBER

Copyright © 2017 Justin Loeber.
Published by Mango Publishing Group, a division of Mango Media Inc.

Cover Design: Roberto Núñez
Layout & Design: Roberto Núñez

Mango is an active supporter of authors' rights to free speech and artistic expression in their books. The purpose of copyright is to encourage authors to produce exceptional works that enrich our culture and our open society.

Uploading or distributing photos, scans or any content from this book without prior permission is theft of the author's intellectual property. Please honor the author's work as you would your own. Thank you in advance for respecting our author's rights.

For permission requests, please contact the publisher at:
Mango Publishing Group
2850 Douglas Road, 3rd Floor
Coral Gables, FL 33134 USA
info@mango.bz

For special orders, quantity sales, course adoptions and corporate sales, please email the publisher at sales@mango.bz. For trade and wholesale sales, please contact Ingram Publisher Services at customer. service@ingramcontent.com or +1.800.509.4887.

The Get Out of Your Own Way Guide to Life: 10 Steps to Shift Gears, Dream Big, Do it Now!

Library of Congress Cataloging-in-Publication number: 2017956444.
ISBN: (paperback) 978-1-63353-647-0, (ebook) 978-1-63353-648-7

BISAC category code:
SEL021000 SELF-HELP / Motivational & Inspirational
OCC019000 BODY, MIND & SPIRIT / Inspiration & Personal Growth

Printed in the United States of America

**I dedicate this book to my late mother,
Elayne Atlas Loeber Papadopoulos,**
who, because of her actions in life,
made the world a better place.

**For
Captain Anthony George Papadopoulos,**
an amazing dad. The best father anyone could ask for.

This book is written for anyone
who feels they can't get out of their own way.

**Some, not all, of the names and stories in this book
have been changed
so that my big ass won't get sued!**

For more information, please visit:
www.GetOutOfYourOwnWayBook.com

Praise for *Get Out of Your Own Way Guide to Life*:

"OMG! Get Out of Your Own Way Guide to Life is a Millennial manifesto! Whether you're a reality star or a loser—it's time for you to get your act together and read Justin's book!"

- Taylor Strecker, Host, SiriusXM Stars Channel 109 "Wake Up with Taylor"

"Enjoy Justin's contemporary jabber and Millennial lingo but do reach beyond that to see, in its essence, that Get Out of Your Way Guide to Life is a heartfelt and valuable guide, filled with sensitive, meaningful words of wisdom and support for all who read it.»

- Peter Yarrow, American Folksinger and Songwriter, Peter, Paul and Mary; Founder, Operation Respect; and co-Author, *Puff the Magic Dragon*

"Often blunt and always irreverent, Loeber's energy and humor crackle off the page as he guides his readers on a tough-love journey of self-discovery. His expert advice and candid revelation of his own unconventional path to business success will be inspiring to anyone who finds themselves adrift and wondering what to do next."

-Jacqueline Deval, VP Publisher, Hearst Books; Author of *Publicize Your Book!* and *Reckless Appetites*

"No matter where you're from, Justin Loeber steps into your world and helps you reach your goals."

- Con Coughlin, Defense Editor and Chief Foreign Affairs Columnist, *The Telegraph*; Author of *Saddam: King of Terror*

"Justin is the king of personal branding and helping one reinvent themselves. This guide is a fantastic roadmap for aligning one to their purpose."

- Jan Strode, President & CEO, CEO Advisors

Foreword

Justin Loeber is a branding and marketing genius. But more than that, he's a deeply wise and funny sage who isn't afraid to say it like it is in order to help people rise to be their best and brightest selves.

Each of us has greatness inside. No matter where we come from or how difficult our pasts may be, our futures can be big, bold, and filled with extraordinary success. Justin believes this to his core (as do I), and in his feisty and fierce book, *Get Out of Your Own Way Guide to Life*, he'll show you how you can drop your shit, own your worth, and step into your true power.

You see, you were built for more. 'Tis true. You have a beautiful purpose whether you know it or not. And you've got the talent and smarts to meet that purpose. Your job is simply to wake up and accept your unique awesomeness so you can get busy living like you really mean it.

Will there be obstacles along the way? Heck yeah. Sometimes they'll come from outside forces, but more often than not they'll creep up from the inside.

I mean, let's face it: we all have negative voices, past experiences, and present distractions that can keep us playing small. Wouldn't it be amazing to learn how to tame that noise and see it for what it really is? Fear. Self-doubt. Illusion.

Can you imagine how strong you'd feel if you learned to treat yourself with the respect and sacredness you deserve? To look your fear in the eye and go for it anyway?

Well, your dreams are asking you to do just that and they require courage. People often think it's confidence that's needed for success, but really, it's courage. And whether you know it or not, you're plenty brave. You just may need some encouragement and tools to help you flex your gutsy muscles.

It's time to be on your own side and have your own back as you navigate your way to your destiny. And with this book, you now have a fabulous and fiery blueprint to help you create your own rules, your own standards, and your own success on *your own* terms.

As a world-renowned performer and a seasoned public relations expert with an extensive background in publishing, Justin has experienced it all. Not only has he had his own incredible journey in front of and behind the spotlight, he's also seen how certain people rise to meet and even exceed their potential—and how others get in their own way.

With Justin's guidance, some of the biggest names in entertainment, politics, sports, literature, and medicine, as well as corporate household brands and so on, have learned how to harness their talent and effectively get their message and mission across to the masses.

Now, you don't have to want to be the next big star to get a boatload of wisdom out of this gem of a book. The lessons learned here will help you with your next job, relationship, friendship, insecurity, or obstacle.

The advice you'll receive is ultimately about living your life to the fullest, no matter what you choose to do with it. And the truth is, we all want to shine brightly in our own little universes. I certainly did.

When I first met Justin, he had been hired by my then-publisher to promote my first book, *Crazy Sexy Cancer Tips*, and my award-winning documentary film, *Crazy Sexy Cancer*. These projects were born out of my own experience as a young woman living with a Stage IV, incurable disease. I often say that as I was looking for the cure, I found my life. Like so many people who experience a serious wake-up call, cancer put life into perspective and helped me focus on what really matters. I learned how to take care of myself and others at the deepest level, to bridge the worlds of western and integrative medicine, and to teach others how to become empowered participants in their well-being.

My simple mission became a global movement that began with Justin's incredible guidance, direction, and support. To say he was a huge part of my success is an understatement. I couldn't have done it without him.

From day one, Justin took me under his glittery wing and taught me how to own my own stage. I was green. I was scared as hell, and I was often so nervous. I didn't think I could do it. But he wouldn't let my negative voices get in my way because he knew I had so much to share with the world (just as you do). So Justin would coach me day and night, take me to every interview, and practice with me what to say, how to steer the interview back to my message if it drifted, and how to just be myself and have fun—no matter what. Then we'd rinse and repeat and get back out there!

Well, the doors flew open and I was booked on every national TV show, including *Oprah*. Thank you, Justin! It's been over a decade since then, and I've met many coaches, trainers, TV executives, publishers, celebrities, and so on. But I always come back to Justin's tools and advice, and I continue to build my brand and my life on my own unique terms.

You have a treasure in your hands. This little book is filled with "wows," "ahas," and a whole lotta love and wisdom. My advice to you: listen. Take what resonates for a spin and give this one glorious life of yours your all. As Justin always tells me, "Get out there and do your fabulous tap dance, baby!"

You've got this.

Peace and possibilities,

—Kris Carr, *New York Times* and #1 Amazon bestselling author and Justin's biggest fan

Table Contents

Introduction

To live a full life is an honor that comes with a responsibility—to yourself. Whether you are a nurse, a landscaper, a pop singer, a philosopher, an artist, a Broadway hoofer, a brain surgeon, a parent, an "A" student, a fashion model, a gas pumper or a deadbeat, we're all here on this Earth for such a brief moment. I have unpacked most—not all—of the baggage that has weighed me down emotionally, which could have potentially stopped me from moving into the next semester of life. As I continue to blow out more and more birthday candles, I have come to conclude that a huge number of us are so busy clicking on some sort of electronic device that we're forgetting about literally looking up, getting out of our own way, and seeing that the life we were given is a gift. Don't get me wrong: I love what electronics stand for, and I'd be a dummy to work in the communications business without embracing it all. I love pizza too; however, if I ate slices and slices of it on a daily basis, I'd be as huge as a helicopter spinning out of control. So it's safe for me to say, here and now, that we are all (as a culture) addicted to electronics—to the point where we're putting ourselves in the passenger's seat, looking down and letting a smartphone do a lot of the work. You've got to admit that for the most part, we're in the infancy stage of this modern electronics boom. The whole thing is really clunky at times—like us, it really can't get out of its own way either. It's trying desperately to be streamlined, but I shudder at how many people have developed physical ailments like "text neck," carpal tunnel, poor eyesight, and disrupted sleep from all these toys.

I promise you in less than ten years, we'll all laugh at what we all went through during the "Wild Wild West" of twenty-first century technology. More importantly, after reading this book, I hope you put down the gadgets and move over to the pilot's chair and literally soar up to the trip of your lifetime.

I'm sorry to break that news to you—especially if you're one of those Millennials or Generation Zers who might live and breathe "glass half empty." Even though in many *marketing* circles I might be past my prime (aka irrelevant), the in-your-face street smarts rulebook I have embraced doesn't include a large-print section for mature audiences. People are people in my book—literally! Because there's no prejudice here, I figured that it was time to pass on some of the in-the-trenches knowledge that I've gained over my more than a few decades of life, to those who might not yet have stepped into their own brighter light—bright enough to understand how precious, quick, and down and dirty *living* is. Yes, it's time.... It's time to understand you've made a very intimate pact with yourself to spend your energy on the "it" that makes you tick. Good or bad, you've made choices that mark you for the moment and could stick and define you forever. And if you don't think you have the "it," I can promise you that you do. After reading this book, I hope you will have the courage, without apology, to find that "extraordinary" in you—the real reason why you're here.

It's time to get out of your own way and make "things" happen.

I thought about writing this book when one Millennial paraded into my office for a job interview in flip-flops and shorts and all tangled up in wires from his earbuds—with such an entitlement issue that I was one step from asking this kid to leave before listening to his spiel. I realized that one Millennial after another was coming into my office, shockingly clueless about what his or her life's purpose is. And many of those considered "older" continue to sashay into my firm as if they saw a ghost of career past—they don't have a clue, either because they still believe they're working in the glorious days of the 80s when everyone and everything seemed to be on steroids and sipping liquid lunches. (For those who don't know, a "liquid lunch" is when you get bombed at lunch on martinis.) Both demographics— under and over thirty—are out of touch with the middle ground that mixes all of our lives together, and impacts how we all communicate with each other—no matter what our ages are. Whatever generation you fit into, please stop being so set in your ways, defeated before you take a risk, jaded, and opinionated about everything.

So, how can this *Get Out of Your Own Way Guide to Life* help you get out of your own way? I've set the book up in ten steps, and at the end of every piece there's a mini "take-a-quiz" with five practical questions and a cheat sheet with answers. I promise you won't feel like you're reading *CliffsNotes*—it's just a few easy-breezy flash questions to encourage you to think further about the subject at hand.

As an added bonus (here's where the big pitch comes into play!), dotted throughout the book are a boatload of my version of "hashtag takeaways." You'll notice that my hashtags are full sentences. On Twitter, #hashtags are just one word or a #ShortPhraseWrittenInCamelCase. But part of my message is that we need to slow down, take a personal mental check, and actually *say* what's going on in our subconscious. It's all about what we mean to say. We can be brief. Our actions should speak louder than words...we should listen to that little voice inside our head, because it is the gut instinct that is usually spot on. So think of my "hashtag takeaways" as if you're cracking open a fortune cookie to reveal "news you can use" at a glance. In reality, it's me bottom-lining a thought for you in the hope that you're listening.

I hope these communication formats in the book are ultimately of value—just like some people read hard books while others like e-versions. I hate it when I buy a book or a ticket to a movie or show, and it sucks—that's money down the drain. I believe the customer is always right. Lemme get back to you if my publisher offers a money-back guarantee if this rant ain't happenin' for ya, OK?

#(Wink, wink.)

#(Insert Smiley Face here.)

Let's show you some sample hashtag takeaways that further describe what the hell is peppered between these pages. Would one of these one-liners describe you?

#She helped the poor escape from the prison camps.

#He didn't believe there was an environmental crisis.

#She was a shopaholic—didn't give a shit about her kids.

GET OUT OF YOUR OWN WAY GUIDE TO LIFE

#He discovered a cure for cancer.

Along with the Ten Steps I will soon be going through with you, and the whole "hashtag" shebang in the book, I will share snippets of my life story—how I saw myself, and see myself now—so that you can use my personal experiences as a thrust towards looking into your history and destiny.

We are in a world that texts, types, reads and speaks in 140 characters or less, with an attention span of a peanut. Boomers like me, who lived in a land that once was truly free from Big Brother meddling in our business, didn't need an app to tell us how to think, how to date, how to be marketed to, and how to communicate. The sad truth is, in the world of the hashtag, it's a real pipe dream if you think the galaxy is going to recite your Wikipedia page every time someone brings your name up— dead or alive. Respectfully, with that kind of mindset, you're slightly delusional from how the world works. If you think that farkakte Facebook is going to create that eerie looped video of memories they're known for *after* you die—hell no, papi! The party is "ovah" when you kick the bucket. Big Bro will press "Delete" because your life has used up way too much cloud storage! What people will remember is *not* your greatest novel or TV series, but a line or two of gossip—that's right, "g-o-s-s-i-p," better known as "potentially fake news"—that they heard about you. ("Did you hear he was a nasty sonofabitch?" "She was a trust fund baby and didn't need to work after all...why didn't she let the talented one take over her position?")

After reading the *Get Out of Your Own Way Guide to Life*, I hope and pray you won't feel the constant need to fit into a life like The Friggen' Joneses. You know The Friggen' Joneses: those "perfect" peeps who feel the need to breathe like, look like, talk like, compete with, and live like everyone else to stay relevant: be accepted. These are people who try and trick you from knowing their real age, because they're afraid no one will aspire to be them any longer.

Ageism (at any age) is so last Tuesday in my book, so I'm not sure what The Friggen' Joneses are worried about. It's only a pain in the butt if we want it to be. For those of us who were alive in the 60s and 70s (two freakin' fantastic decades, I might add), it seems as if the marketers of today feel the need to keep us locked up at the Woodstock Music Festival, continually playing a Janis Joplin track that no person under thirty-eight has ever heard. These marketing geniuses are desperate to split us up into "demographics" and niche everyone out as if we're all products, separated up and down the aisles of a supermarket. What would the world be like if cold cereal was sold on the shelf next to laundry detergent? As long as each box is closed, that wouldn't be a problem.

Many younger Debbie Downers, who think their dewy age gives them the right to act like zombies (because their parents divorced and no one had the time to make them great tuna fish sandwiches growing up), pooh-pooh chances presented right in front of them and waste time with excuses, most likely out of fear. Sadly, they spend way too many hours stuck in pause mode, glued to reality TV, violent video games, and celebrity banter—or, dare I say, addicted to their smartphones. (There I go again about electronics. More to come.) To many, it's easy to "click out and tune in" to someone else's life (like the

Kardashians, like the "Real Housewives," like the judges on "Shark Tank," and like all the great athletes and superstars), because while you vicariously spend their money, or pretend you're living in their success-ilicious private compounds, you don't have time to focus on your own shit.

Nowadays, instead of taking a walk on the beach, needlepointing, playing football, reading a book or newspaper, or playing Frisbee, a lot of us spend our "anytime" on the white noises of electronics and their constant nagging updates— anything to avoid facing the fact that, perhaps, time is ticking by without the sun shining in our direction. Some of us are climbing up a mountain called "Extraordinary," and some are going down a twisted road called "Time Waster." That doesn't mean you can't binge on trashy TV or run to watch the latest pop star's live performance on the Grammy Awards. C'mon— we do *need* life balance; however, balance means that when the show is over, it's time for you to turn it off, look the fuck *up* from the dating app, and get the blood flowing again, people... with those who don't lie about their age and actually look like their thumbnail pics.

#The new boob tube is the smartphone.

#At times, social media should be called *anti*-social media.

#Social media is really just another thousand channels on a TV remote.

#If you'd rather watch a traditional sitcom on your iPad and get "text neck," so be it.

After hours and hours of electronic and anti-social overload, what do YOU want to be known for at the end of the day?

#He was a creep shoplifting Prada bags at Macy's.

or

#She was a hero who saved an old lady from an attacker.

Making a 180-degree life turn is not that hard; all you need to do is have the ability to keep it moving in a positive direction and open up to the possibility that you deserve a better experience.

Like the person who goes from shoplifter to caregiver, you can absolutely, unequivocally transition from a negative past to a positive, uber-successful future. Reinvention is amazing. You really don't need anyone other than yourself to approve the change you want to redefine your life—good, bad or indifferent. Through the anecdotes in this book, I truly hope you will gain the strength to be honest and intimate with yourself, so that when it's time for the artisans to start etching an epitaph onto your mausoleum, *you* and your friends will have so many great things to say about you that even your enemies will even applaud!

#Roll up your sleeves and get scrappy about your life.

#Talking honestly about yourself can be inspirational.

Lemme get this party going, and let me start to tell you my story—you'll find it ain't hard for me.

Way back in the late 70s and 80s, I was a bit of an ultra-creative ball of fire...a self-involved, overly sensitive twentysomething. But after going through many humbling experiences—including losing my biological parents, losing an inheritance, losing four recording contracts (as a pop singer), going through two cancer health scares and losing friends to tragic illnesses—now, at my age, I live, without apology, in a luscious color of everything. I crave to always be challenged. One side of me wants to kick off my shoes and eat some bonbons, but the other side says, light the fiyah and keep it moving, grandpa!

**#Breathe like a dragon who is
going to be honored for Chinese New Year.**

People often tell me I have a quirky outlook on life and an inspiring backstory, which I hope is a solid platform for handing out some heartfelt advice in this book. In my career in public relations and now with PR and social media, I have represented hundreds of fascinating people—I've had the luck and good fortune to work with some of the greats: superstar athletes like Michael Jordan; recording legends like Peter, Paul and Mary, Carly Simon, Judy Collins, Neil Sedaka and Kenny Loggins; actors like Olympia Dukakis, Blair Underwood, and Marlo Thomas; movie producers like Linda Obst; models like Cindy Crawford; reality stars like Snooki; iconic sex kittens like Pamela Anderson; political prisoners like Ingrid Betancourt; senior prime ministers like Lee Kuan Yew of Singapore; newscasters like Dan Rather; attorneys like Gloria

Allred and Raoul Felder; brands like The Elf on the Shelf and Halo Purely for Pets; Latina powerhouses like Celia Cruz; extraordinary wellness warriors like Kris Carr; heartfelt doctors like Andrew Weil and Neal Barnard; moral philosophers like Peter Singer; and literary stars like Paolo Coelho, Leon Uris, Diane McKinney-Whetstone, and Mitch Albom, just to name a few. I have had the honor of stepping into each one's unique definition of "normal." Normal or not, seeing some of these people reveal their "deck of cards" has given me the perspective to understand parts of my life that either work or don't.

**#Share your deck of cards in order to
help others find their purpose.**

I want to expose you to the fire that burns inside my clients' bellies, giving them the impetus to persevere. I am humbly grateful for the opportunity to work with such inspirational people—whether for a few months or for several years—and I want to thank them for helping me find one of my personal missions in life. When people sign up for public relations and social media services, they are typically at a quasi-mystical level that drives them to only want to bring their "A" game and to be sitting in the front row when the curtain goes up and the stage explodes. After repping famous people, I now know, and you will too, that:

**#Everyone can afford a ticket to their own
award-winning performance of a lifetime.**

The public relations and social media "show" that my staff and I proudly perform each day requires a talent for becoming a client's messenger to his or her own message—holding up a mirror and asking, "Just who are you? What do you bring to the table? Why should anyone care? I want to help you press the accelerate button on the story of your life. From this page forward, it's just you and me, navigating our plusses and minuses together. (I'll show you mine if you show me yours!) When it's time for people to consider you for work, friendship, or play, this handbook and (at least some of) my philosophies will help you, I promise. As I hinted above, one of the biggest secrets to living a full life is that you don't always need to follow the rules—or struggle to fit into anyone else's standards to be successful.

#It takes a lotta guts to dream big and take bold steps.

# # #

Back to my life: I didn't start out as bold as I am today. As a kid, I was so shy and quirky—like a flower that needed to be watered in order not to shrivel up.

**#If you're a hot mess, take ownership of it—
and either fix it or wallow in *paranoid*.**

When people would call my house, I sounded like a squeaky little girl and would get so upset when the phone rang that I'd refuse to speak. (It's funny that I now own a company with the word "mouth" in it.) At the age of four, someone shot a cap gun in my eye and I was rushed to the hospital, blinded for hours. Doctors thought I would never see again. Overnight, my mom became uber-overprotective. In response to her panic,

I built an emotional wall around myself, reinforced with tons of stuffed animals sitting by my side in fantasy. Then, at the age of eight, I had an ear abscess so "dire" that a doctor told my parents I should live my entire life in a plastic bubble to avoid more infections. Michael Jackson had nothing on me, trust me. (Happily, my parents didn't follow that wacky doc's recommendation—but then again, it was the 1960s and there were a lot of those wack-a-doodles out there, trust me.)

Before long, my emotional wall morphed into a "wall of weight." I was the first person in third grade to break one hundred pounds. When I made a mistake in class at South Mountain Elementary School in South Orange, New Jersey, one teacher, Mrs. Ernst, put a dunce cap on my head and paraded me around to every classroom in the building, telling everyone that I was stupid and a dummy. So, you can imagine why I carried around a lot of baggage and became chronically shy and obese. Here I was at nine years old, unlike everyone else, and at times I felt obsolete. (I was in my twenties when my mom told me she threatened to poke Mrs. Ernst's eyes out if she ever put a dunce cap on me again—I wondered why Mrs. Ernst was suddenly being nice to me!)

In fourth grade, still waddling down the hallways like a roly-poly, the other kids would scream in between classes, "Fat Larry wants to marry Miss Vancarry!" Yes, my first name is Larry—Lawrence, actually. My full name is Lawrence Justin Loeber. My mom had visions of me going to Lawrence*ville*, a college preparatory boarding school in New Jersey, but I wanted to be comfy-cozy, chubby Larry who was born in NYC and grew up in Jersey, thank you very much! (And no, I wasn't named after the prep school.)

#My mom wanted me to go to boarding school— all I wanted was to go to a diner.

I fell further into the "lack of confidence" category—until high school. Hit with the performance bug and armed with potent fantasies—picturing myself singing with Louie Armstrong (while he sang "Hello Dolly"), James Brown, Stevie Wonder, Average White Band, Earth, Wind & Fire, Melba Moore, Rufus & Chaka Khan (my dog Rufus is named after the band), Marvin Gaye, The Brothers Johnson, Ohio Players, Aretha Franklin, The Isley Brothers, Bette Midler, and Barbra Streisand (a huge inspiration for me!), among others—I convinced my parents to allow me to take the bus (from the Jersey suburbs to Manhattan!) three times a week for lessons in singing, dancing and acting.

#When the chips are down, start tap-dancing and sing pop music!

I'd finally found something that fit me. Once I stepped on the stage, I owned it—without analyzing the fear that supposedly came with performing. As soon as I hit puberty, I morphed into this kid who could sing the shit out of anything. I was absorbing the creative spirit inside me, as if I were a Scrub Daddy "happy" sponge sopping up water on a kitchen counter. Because I had these pipes that could belt out a tune all the way from Jersey to Times Square (really!) I had the honor of being accepted to and attending the Manhattan School of Music Preparatory

School for voice and the HB Studio for drama—not to mention the Alvin Ailey School for modern dance, Henry LeTang for tap, and Jo-Jo Smith and Phil Black for jazz (where I learned my moves with the other JLo—Jennifer Lopez—who also studied at Phil's). In those days, the doors of the greats were wide open, and for about $2.50 a class, one could walk in and learn from them. My parents also let me apply for the National Music Camp in Interlochen, Michigan; not only was I accepted, but I stayed and "starred" in shows for three summers. At camp, I was a ballsy and competitive SOB. One year, I was the first person in the state of Michigan to come down with chicken pox (as a teenager—not attractive), right at the time when campers were auditioning to be in the big productions of the summer. Unhappy with being quarantined for the pox and sitting on the sidelines, I "demanded" that the directors come to the infirmary to audition me behind a window (because I was still infectious). I'd be damned if I was going to watch others on a stage that should be starring me!

#Don't let a little infection stand in the way of your spotlight.

After those great summers at NMC in Interlochen, I studied more and more drama, dance and voice in NYC. During one summer, I dropped sixty pounds eating cottage cheese and lettuce while I was learning how to tap, getting my vocal chords in shape, and learning how to act. Talk about coming of age! What I lost in fat, I gained in confidence, shedding a bit of that pompous asshole-ness and becoming a nicer person to be around. *Adios,* squeaky little girl! (And a big *adios* to my biological father, who met a waitress and her older daughter on the highway, divorced my mom, and apparently moved to Florida with this brood.) Incidentally, I learned my dad moved to Florida when I dialed his number and the auto-attendant said, "The number you have reached has been changed...." Really classy, dad.

#When you lose weight, you celebrate.

#When an uninterested parent leaves you, you celebrate.

Everything didn't go my way, though. Fast forward to my first year at NYU Undergraduate Drama. I was accepted to the school after my audition, but then rejected because my SAT scores were abysmal: 390 (Math) and 420 (English). (OK, so I'm tremendously flawed when it comes to taking standardized tests.) I got some help from a family friend who knew someone in Admissions, and simultaneously I pitched many of my teachers, from first grade through high school (except for Mrs. Ernst), to write me a character reference. Voila! I guess this was the first time I became my own publicist. I was re-accepted to the university. Through the school's undergraduate drama program, I was lucky to study acting under the great Stella Adler; but the academic curriculum I chose to earn some sort of degree (which, BTW, I didn't get) sucked for me. I wanted out. I didn't have the patience to go through four years of the "I'm not sure why I'm here" mode that many college students seem to go through.

So I dropped out of NYU and shifted gears again, both professionally and geographically. My focus turned from acting to recording pop music...but not in New York! After seeing an

MTV interview with the Stray Cats—an 80s rockabilly band whose members kept yowling about how they "couldn't get arrested" in the States, but were all the rage in the UK—I set my sights on becoming a pop recording artist in England. Sadly, my dad (the one who exited stage left for an "ultra-fabulous life" in The Sunshine State), refused to help support my leaving NYU in favor of "career" in show business. That was fine by me (no hard feelings!) because my will to be a pop recording artist superseded my biological father's approval.

#If your dream doesn't fit into someone else's, screw them.

When the plane landed in the UK, I put my gut life strategy in motion. I said to myself that I was going to get a recording contract before my visa expired. I was going to pretend that I was Mickey Rooney with Judy Garland, put on a show out of my garage, and never take the word "no" for an answer. I decided I was going to use my "Americanisms" as a plus—to be a bit odd to the Brits and become a character in my own real-life performance.

So, here's the wrap-up: one day I was Fat Larry, the next I was a college dropout, and the next I left for England and morphed into "Larry Loeber," the first signed solo artist on Gary "Cars" Numan's record label, Numa, debuting with a single called "Shivers Up My Spine," which was starting to get airplay on BBC's Radio 1 in London. Friends asked me why I didn't call it "Shivers *Down* My Spine." Yup, even back in the 80s, I always thought up, not down—and my visualization of having a recording contract in hand before my Virgin Atlantic flight took off from Heathrow to JFK really paid off.

My dreams continued to grow: while I was recording the demos that eventually turned into singles, I almost passed out when I saw the sign "Sting" in the next room at Shepperton Recording Studios in England. And that's not all: imagine my reaction at meeting the likes of the late George Michael, who was on the cusp of becoming a household name with his band, "Wham!" Within a few months, I conceptualized and filmed a music video for "Shivers..," which incidentally, a fan posted on YouTube. *Oy.* (In the video, I put on a turban and Raybans, flew around in a magic carpet, and the rest is up to you to find out!) This was back when MTV was a network that only played those things.) I was recording more songs, including a rendition of Norman Greenbaum's "Spirit in the Sky," for an album. I also got word that I was to be one of the openers on Numan's multicity "Berserker Tour" across the UK. The deal was for me to perform to the backing tracks of my upcoming album, alone, and in front of the proscenium, which in many of the arenas, were only a few feet deep and wide.

On that tour, I had a lightbulb moment—another visualization—but this time, it didn't include Rooney or Garland. It happened at a gig (I think it was in Wales), where the stage was at the same level as the mezzanine, so high up you couldn't see those in the orchestra unless you looked way down. According to the venue, if the audience hated my performance, they would literally throw glass beer bottles at me—hence the reason why the stage was so high up. What the fuck?! Being hit by hurling glass in front of thousands wouldn't be a nice welcome for an American (or anyone), I'd say, and seemed much worse than hearing that I was Fat Larry who wanted to marry Miss Vancheri. In fact, getting hit in the head by a glass beer bottle is, to me, the absolute most humiliating thing in public that could ever happen to anyone. My pop star dreams got a nasty wake-up call—but I can proudly say that I would never, ever, ever get a beer bottle thrown at me. From that day forward, I figured out a way to always dodge the glass beer bottle—on the stage, with my clients, and generally in life.

One day, I heard the news that Mike Read, a famous DJ at Radio One in London—the guy who started playing "Shivers…" across the airwaves, had wanted to interview me. (Apparently, the interview was predicated on Gary Numan joining in, but I heard he declined.) Hmmmm.

Just as if you'd turned off your radio, my music career in London abruptly came to a halt because of a stupid work permit debacle. I didn't realize that when I was offered the chance to open for Numan's tour and the label gave me the necessary paperwork to do so, I needed to leave the country for a few days and enter back in with said permit so that the officials at the airport could stamp a date on it. (What? Yeah, I was confused too.) Airport security said I was in breach of my original entry as a tourist: I took a job (as a pop recording artist) away from an English citizen. But I had the work permit, I just hadn't reentered to get it stamped! What a shock. God help any Brit (whom I apparently "stole" a job from) who decides to write another single called, "Shivers Up My Spine!" Really? Apparently, it didn't concern anyone at Numa because no one from the label, including Gary, showed up to bail me out of this mess. I was really heartbroken and totally frustrated. (Honestly, I think Numan was more interested in flying antique airplanes than running his record label, leaving the task at hand to his mum Beryl, and his dad, Tony—genuinely nice people who seemed to be a bit naïve—like me—when it came to working in the music business.) Who runs a record label, hears that one of their acts is stuck at customs at the airport, and doesn't bother to simply show up—or send a rep. After being "denied entrance" from London (the police, though, gave me seven days to pack up and clear out—I felt like one of Donald Trump's illegal Mexican aliens getting deported after jumping over a wall to make a dream come true),

Within seven days of the ordeal at Heathrow, I was flown back to the States with no place to live. Before leaving for the UK, I had sublet my apartment to the manager of Wayland Flowers and Madame, a famous and flamboyant ventriloquist and his puppet—and no way was that manager leaving my roost prematurely. (I'll talk more about this towards the end of the book.) Not only did I lose my techno-pop recording career, but I was shut out of my apartment and was destined to sleep on my parents' couch (my parents this time around consisted of my mom and my stepdad Tony who you'll get to know later)— they were the only ones to open their doors to me. Hit hard by that fact, I was in a deep shock and depression.

#Devastating moments are just a test for you to decide whether or not your life choices are worth fighting for.

Six years after *L'exit* (short for Larry's exit from Britain), I was now armed with two more dance record contracts in America— one with Vinylmania (where the famous dance music producer, the late Sergio Munzibai, remixed my song, "Those Words," originally recorded in London), the other with Emergency Records (where renegade dance producer, Freddy Bastone, remixed my original, "Love Me or Leave Me"). According to my Emergency contract, I had the right to approve my mixes; however, at the time I was told when to show up at the studio, the fucker had mixed my record already, and in a few hours I apparently morphed from a techno-pop recording artist to a Latin Freestyle singer. Don't get me wrong. If I could have pulled off the Latin vibe like Ricky Martin, you would not have heard me complain. What would you think if U2's music was mixed into Country? I hope I rest my case. What a branding nightmare. Both singles permeated the New York dance clubs in the 80s. And that's not quite all of the music drama: I later negotiated another recording contract, with music legend Sid Bernstein and his New York Music Company (Sid told me he brought The Beatles and The Rolling Stones, among others, to America)— that contract went by the wayside; and another contract with Buddy Allen Management (which represented The Spinners, Stacy Lattisaw, and Brenda K. Starr, the 80s dance recording artist who gave Mariah Carey her first break as a backup singer, plus more) proved another waste of time.

#Why is the music business so complicated and dysfunctional?

With all the complications that surrounded the music business and me, none of them compare to what happened on the self-proclaimed "last night" of my music career—which literally ended with a bang. At my last gig, at a club called 1018 (later known as The Roxy) in NYC, someone shot a gun—not a cap gun—above the crowd. I came to realize that the gunshot was meant to be a spiritual "period" at the end of my music sentence—and by "sentence," boy, I mean it felt like a prison sentence. It was time to blow the dust off my wounded lyrical soul and move onward (Another shift in gear.) I was absolutely done with record labels that screwed me and with snaky club owners who didn't pay me. I had an urge to surround myself with supportive and trustworthy people who didn't care about which bass drum sound supported my backing tracks. I finally turned off the music, at least for now, because none of these opportunities paid the landlord's rent.

#When the work don't pay, do not stay.

Even though that gunshot closed the door to my music, it opened the door to reinvention. As part of it, I was on a road to switching my middle name for my first (which I finally brought to unofficial fruition in 1990, when I hosted a "Just Say Justin" party for my friends and relatives).

While simultaneously recording music in the US, I needed cold, hard cash; for seven years, I landed at NYC's MTA (Metropolitan Transportation Authority) Data Center, working as a temp who typed on a Wang word processor. During that period I was still taking a ton of dance classes, just as one of my buddies asked me to fill in for him as a go-go dancer at a club called Danceteria in NYC. That was the weirdest thing I ever did; however, not surprisingly, the nightly pay was more than I made in the music business. After my experience with the MTA, I spent fifteen years in the restaurant business, working my way up from host (at Tavern-on-the-Green, where my manager, the soon-to-be-legendary NYC restauranteur, Drew Nieporent, managed me), and waiting tables (at such places as The Duck Joint, where I served the ravishing, Catherine Deneuve), to general management at the now defunct Triplets Romanian Steakhouse in NYC, an old-time Jewish eatery. Triplets was run by a set of triplets who were separated at birth—two of whom ended up at the same college nonetheless, serving up dinner and dancing as a belly-dancer wiggled around for tips. It was a show put on by the waiters—and me. So the waiters sang show tunes, and I (awkwardly) sang my techno-British-ish pop tunes to my backing tracks, playing to an audience that included, on every Jewish holiday, none other than one of the great music mavens of all time, Clive Davis, who would bring his family. (For anyone who hasn't heard of Clive, please do your research.) Here I was, a self-served, washed-up recording artist almost no one knew, singing my disco dance hits to a crowd one step removed from the Borscht Belt circuit. Unfortunately, even though Clive Davis coincidentally happened to be a childhood friend of a family friend, I was not destined to be discovered during the High Holidays. The famous record producer (rightfully so) focused on eating his chicken soup with matzah balls rather than listening to my rendition of "Spirit in the Sky." (I loved singing that song at this Jewish place with the lyric, "You gotta have a friend in Jesus!")

As fast as the waitstaff hustled at Triplets, I realized the restaurant gigs were bringing me back to my "Fat Larry" days— where I was constantly surrounded by food. That's when I seized the next 180 degree opportunity—in publishing. At the age of thirty-three, and taking a forty thousand dollar annual pay cut from Triplets, I took a temp job answering phones in the publicity department of Villard, a division of Random House. I was searching for a career change. I tinkered with the thought of designing baseball caps of all things; however, my friend and awesome publicist, Sharyn Rosenblum, presented the PR temp job to me. She and her boss, publishing dynamo Jacqueline Deval, weren't necessarily looking for someone "invested" in the "opportunity"—they simply needed a body to pick up the phone and say, "Hello," by the second ring. This gig was a little "administrative," but I did not leave it every night smelling like chopped liver or singing to thugs with guns! I remember Sharyn silently suffering because I was so awkward in the traditional workplace—Jacqueline got a kick out of me, I think. I had never worked at a publishing company, let alone read a book since reading *1984* in high school. (Incidentally, 1984 was the year I was performing in London— yet surprisingly, wasn't mentioned in Orwell's book.)

The people in publishing seemed a helluva lot more honest than the musicians and kitchen staff I had encountered—even if the publishing set in general were a bit snooty and very impressed with their college degrees. For whatever reason, no one in the industry ever questioned my educational background; I guess I looked like someone who went to school—albeit just high school and one (or was it two?) years at NYU.

#Typing well, without grammatical errors, can get you into publishing. (At least in those days.)

That's how I broke into the book business—seizing an opportunity with bright eyes open and without a college degree or any experience other than an interest to learn, a passion for showing up on time, an ability to type documents, a knack for organizing storerooms of books, some fun stories about performing music in London, and a will to see beyond a temporary position. Less than thirteen years later, I ended my corporate publishing career as a Senior Vice President, Executive Marketing and Publicity Director for Regan Media (run by the colorful Judith Regan), after enjoying other great job opportunities at William Morrow, Broadway Books (Bantam Doubleday Dell), Ecco (HarperCollins), Running Press, HarperCollins, and Atria (Simon and Schuster).

During my time at William Morrow, I saw firsthand just how powerful PR can work for some. Maybe you've read, or at least heard of, the Penguin Group's best-selling book, *The Color of Water: A Black Man's Tribute to His White Mother* by James McBride. I was surprised to learn that McBride's mother was my mom's first cousin, a fact which my mom learned when she heard an interview on NPR that had been set up by the author's book publicist. Through the power of this PR interview, McBride's mission for his book—reuniting his mother with her relatives—was accomplished.

After all my colorful corporate PR opportunities, I took another bold leap and launched my own PR firm—from my bedroom. In 2016, Mouth Public Relations celebrated its tenth anniversary in business; in March 2017, we rebranded to become "mouth: digital and public relations." Now operating out of offices in lower Manhattan, Mouth has represented over five hundred clients in the "entertainment," "beauty/health/wellness," "nonprofit," "food/nutrition," "consumer/lifestyle," "wedding," "B2B," "author," and "social media" categories, to name a few.

It seems as if the Higher Power said to my mom (before I came out of her womb), "This one's going to go on a quirky path, but he'll be a late bloomer and everything will be alright." Whether I knew it or not, over my career's twists and turbulence I built up an arsenal of street smarts, communication skills, gut instincts, a talent for rebounding and surviving, and a keen sense of how to stay relevant without getting a beer bottle thrown at me. I learned how to get out of my own way.

So, leveraging all the moxie I've built up, here's my promise to you: I can help you come to terms with whatever is hindering and haunting you from finding your close-up. Are you tired of sitting back, fed up with reading and watching other people's success stories cut and pasted over the Internet? Are you at the point where you're not going to accept that life is passing you by? You have been a bored audience member for way too long, but now it's your turn to shine bright.

#If the people around you are holding you back, say goodbye and walk out.

If your conscience tells you, *"The only thing holding me back is myself, and I'm tired of getting in my own way,"* listen. Then, do something about it. *Walk on.*

If you really want to throw out the notion you must be perfect to be successful or let go of the myth you have to have some special talent to dream big, I promise you will love reading onward.

No one gets a free pass to live another hundred years just because they're a Clinton or a Trump or because they won an Oscar. Our clocks tick in sync with every human being, no matter who and where they come from. And that's also the crux of the *Get Out of Your Own Way Guide to Life*: to understand that, when all is said and done, we are all blips on a screen with lives that can be filmed in Technicolor or in a grainy black & white—*it's our choice*. In all reality, our lives that we have worked so hard or so little on can be summed up in a line or two that our family can etch in a tombstone once we have passed. But before we croak and bite the big one, let's work on spinning the storyline differently—especially since we're alive and not ready for anyone to write a sympathy card with our names on it just yet.

If I can carve out a slice of personal success, you can too. I want to encourage you to bask in your own kaleidoscope, and I don't want your jaded conscience to edit your fortune either. Living a life in color might still sound a bit bullshitty, but why should you (or anyone) apologize for tooting your own horn if you really, really know deep down in your heart that the horn you're blowing rings true?

#It is NOT a crime to admit you want to be happy.

Aren't you and the life you are living worth it all? Now it's time to make the donuts. Take a breath and strap yourself into the roller coaster, because you're going to have a great ride. Please read on.

—Justin Loeber

Step One:

Dream Big!

Let me start you off with a big bang (and not the kind I saw at Club 1018).

Draw the curtain up and listen closely:

Dream big, my friends. Do it. Go higher than high.

Don't listen to the doubters, and don't fall in with the "Negative Nellie" crowds that don't want you to succeed. Knock those doubting, bobble-headed booby traps you call "friends" off their spring, and get focused on *you*. It takes as much energy to dream as small as a pea as it does to dream as big as Mount Everest. Dreaming big gives you the gas to drive your emotional car up out of the pitfalls of your own way—it's also a roadmap to rise up, get over yourself, and stop the doubt that has held you in suspended animation.

#Dream big and let the sun finally shine on the person you were born to be.

Take a breath, look up, and, without apology, dream really big and bold. I promise I'll make this step and exercise as entertaining and thoughtful as I have the capacity to: you will not only rise above the road to nowhere on which you've been stalled, but you'll also learn a lot about yourself—good and bad—along the way. This is all about living in the now, at your maximum creative and thoughtful threshold. This is all about making every precious day matter—getting out of your own way, because you never know when today might be the last day you'll have the freedom to start fresh and try again tomorrow.

Speaking of freedom…I live in America, "the land of the free, and home of the brave," to quote "The Star-Spangled Banner." Over the course of my life, I've grown to be brave enough to celebrate my freedom to follow my passions and survival instinct, from acting, dancing, and music, to "Wang'ing" office work at the MTA, slinging hash in restaurants, working in publishing, and now, to being my own boss.

#It's not hard, but it takes a lot of work to go from Point A (working as a temp) to Point B (owning a company).

If you're lucky enough to live in a free society with a boundless ceiling for success, why not work that luck to your advantage? Are you squandering your freedom and losing an opportunity to dream big and act bold because the idea of taking a risk is too painful to contemplate? OK, so you might have had a rotten childhood and a wasted adolescence. Stop blaming your parents, your teachers, or the government. Get over the obstacles in your path, and start taking the leaps to make your ideas matter now. If you want something here and now, put on your adult diapers and stop dribbling. And if you're a Millennial, for God's sake, stop playing the entitled victim—that role has already been filled with the hippie-dippy set who never were able to fit into society because they smoked way too much weed. Defy your generation and act older (and bolder) than your age so that you can get out of your own way and aspire to greatness. Hang in there! If your bright ideas have merit, you're gonna do really, really well because people will take notice.

Here's a thought: so what if your big dream tanks? So what if you fall flat on your face? Remember my washed-up recording career? I had the guts to miss those flying beer bottles in the UK—use that visual as a way to keep *your* ass on the straight and narrow. If you can visualize glass flying towards you, I promise that all of a sudden you'll be awake, alive, and animated enough to get out of the way! If you're in a situation you know is used up—let's say living at home with a lot of unnecessary control over you, or sitting there later in life on the unemployment line—the first step to getting out of your own way is really to just get up, get cracking and rekindle your inner *zhuzh*! Yes, it *is* as easy as that. Get *up*. Get *out. Sing another song*, for Christ's sake! I don't want you to be strapped into a wheelchair at eighty, wondering "what if" you had done this or that when you were younger—or, worse, regretting that you didn't try something simply out of fear. Do you?

**#Go cold turkey and change your attitude immediately.
Yes, it's easy.**

A few years ago, I was naked, doubled over in tears (in the shower!), afraid that my business was tanking. At the time of this personal implosion, my company was more than six years old, and it was the first time that not just one, but *four* clients reneged on their payments, and the first time I sent customers to "collections." Talk about fear: I entered into the first quarter of the next year with only a four thousand dollar float and four employees to pay. Trust me when I tell you, it's not that attractive for a guy with a shaved head to cry in the shower— but it can be very cathartic. At that guttural moment, I was forced to come to terms with my fear: *What would be the worst thing that could happen if my business crumbled?* As my pity party subsided, I came to realize there was absolutely nothing to worry about. Really.

It's not that my business isn't vulnerable to suffering down years. Nearly every business is. But my waterworks of panic got in the way of thinking clearly, which paid off big time. To get a grip on this ground zero moment, all I needed to do was "stop," take a breath," and visualize rock bottom and come to grips with whether or not it's as bad as it could be.

**#If the bottom of the barrel isn't so bad,
why spend unnecessary minutes waddling down yonder?**

Yes, my business could indeed close down without notice (you've gotta have a huge dose of humility when you own a digital and PR company), but I realized that what could potentially be a catastrophe for others wasn't, for me, that horrible after all. If my company crashed, I came to the lightbulb moment of clarity: the worst thing that could happen is that I would have to sell my home, rent a studio apartment (perhaps with a roommate or two), and become a waiter again—something I actually loved doing from time to time before my work in publishing.

#Boo-hoo. I might have to sell my home in favor of renting.

Why isn't this fallback career as bad as it sounds? The bottom line: exercise and cold, hard cash! When you wait on tables, you literally work your ass off running a marathon during your shift. It's no secret that the good waiters leave every day with a wad of tips—as opposed to accumulating cellulite sitting in an office waiting for a headhunter to call. Realizing that my rock bottom wasn't so rocky after all, I was able to squelch a fear that had been holding me hostage—for years. I tricked my brain into thinking that fear of failure was an impetus to do a better job.

#Bawling over the fear of having to kiss my business goodbye was a time-suck.

#Landlords and banks don't care where the mortgage or rent comes from—it just needs to be paid.

Sophia was a friend who moved from the Dominican Republic to the US, trying to rebuild the same career she had in her homeland in her new land. She spent a lot of time mourning the fact that she had lived the high life back home but had nothing to show for it now. What Sophia didn't grasp at first was that, thanks to the Internet, she could indeed keep some of her fancy clients from her hinterland and still work with them virtually while founding a new frontier. Her rock bottom moment forced her to realize:

#Instead of mourning that one door was closing, with the Internet she could open BOTH doors and let clients come in from all over.

47

To get to that realization, she needed to talk through the fear—out loud—with a trusted friend: me. As a supportive and objective listener, I helped my friend determine what her fear was all about and what the creative alternatives could be. After a few back-and-forths, bantering ideas and strategies with each other, Sophia came to understand that what might seem like a scary storyline in her head was really a bare-bones plot she hadn't thought through.

#Empty, fearful noises in the brain are deafening.

Getting back to America's national anthem...on many levels, we really do live freely in a country that's home to smart, strong, and pretty damn brave people who get ahead, mainly because they are passionate and want to be successful without hurting others on their rise up the ladder. True, some people are snakes who will do anything to stomp on you, squelch your spirit, and hijack the limelight away from you—you all know who you are. With all the websites, cameras, and telemarketers sucking our personal information away from us, it's really hard to protect your personal and emotional deck of cards without someone wanting to steal your identity. We're all in a catch-22, because we have to put ourselves out there in order to get something back. When it comes to your dream, my advice would be to let the flood gates open strategically, without sharing your life story with every "nice" person who comes your way.

#It's time for you to create your own success story to tell!

To raise awareness for your dream, you've got to cast a wide net out there, across all platforms. Since there are so many brands, products, corporations, etc. vying for people's attention, you have to go big to get a return. And no one needs to know you only have a four thousand dollar float or a budget for ramen noodles. At this stage of the game, do you want to feel "less than," simply because someone has more money in the bank, more college degrees from a stable of Ivy League schools, more ideas to boast about, and more designer shoes in their closet? Who cares? Again, the broken record in me says, "Who has time to worry about The Friggen' Joneses?" There will always be someone who is richer and hotter, someone who is smarter and taller, and someone who has found the secret to a great invention. (BTW, check out www.CarCane.com for an example. What a great idea for those who need a lift! Haha.)

Let those who are successful have their moment, would you please? And stop feeling sorry for yourself while you vicariously experience someone else's lottery win. Their moment is theirs. It's great karma to congratulate others because positive energy is infectious—it opens the door to you. Visualize your dream. If you've ever gone to a psychic, they'll tell your spiritual team, "Come out, come out, wherever you are!"—and when they do, don't be shy. Ask your ghostly cheerleaders for what you want. See it. Feel it. It's going to happen if you believe that you're worthy of the request. You can—and you will—have your own moment. So, dream big! Then, strategize and rehearse until it's lean and mean, focused and clear. Sum up your dream in a few lines so that prospective supporters can understand it, right on the spot. Once you have your story down pat, all you need to do is find the best and most appropriate audience to *listen* to your life's anthem.

#Applaud someone else's success. Get cracking with yours.

#Rehearse your ass off before you go out there and pitch.

If you're a playwright, work out the synopsis of your story before pitching producers. If you're an aspiring English teacher, make sure you fill out everything on the job application (without any typos) before speaking with the principal. Work out all the pertinent stuff about you ("Who" are you? "What" are you presenting? "Why" are you the one to get this big order?) Rehearse what you'd say, how you'd say it and to whom—*before* you break down the doors and ask for something. The "rehearsal" period is very important because it's the prep time you need to home in on what I call your "nightclub act." We all have one. It's the elevator pitch we tell people when they ask us who we are, and all that goes with it. Rehearsal is the time when you can really be honest with yourself to see what does and doesn't work in your presentation. You will be amazed at how much more confident you'll be when you are prepared.

#Preparation = confidence.

Why not emulate at least one real trait celebrities possess? I'm not one who thinks that celebs are the be-all and end-all of everything that represents success; however, because I've repped plenty of them, there are a few things that go with the territory of being a celebrity that I would like to share with you.

They love to hobnob with other successful people and pitch their ideas to the top of the ladder, rather than keep pitching the person who doesn't make the decisions. Genuine celebs take the elevator straight to the penthouse; they do not wallow in the lobby and stuff themselves into an over-packed elevator to get an answer. In the movies, it takes as much energy to talk to the Wizard as it does to the Munchkins. If you're afraid to look behind the curtain and come face-to-face with whoever holds the power, you are simply setting yourself up for failure. Agree? (BTW, if you have no idea who the Wizard is, watch *The Wizard of Oz*—the original Judy Garland classic.) Seriously though, fear of going to the top is a form of self-sabotage. The top decision-makers might not actually be the ones you need to convince; however, if they are, avoiding them chips away at your self-confidence. That cowardly action shows that you don't think you deserve to spend time with people in power. Unless you can breathe in and taste the notion of hobnobbing with the successful, you're wasting precious tick-tock time.

I call this the "Madonna" factor. You remember Madonna, the original "Material Girl?" (God bless her. We're the same age.) That phenomenally successful recording artist was never afraid of putting her dream into *drive*—and she still isn't. Knowing that even though she might not be the most talented singer, songwriter, or dancer, she understood her worth and went straight for the jackpot, regardless of whether or not The Friggen' Joneses believed in her. Madonna understands the definition of "opportunist" and always goes for it. She doesn't care what Millennials think about her age. Madonna remains focused on living in her spotlight.

#Madonna defies ageism. What can you defy?

As you read in the intro, I left NYU for a "chance" of becoming a recording artist in London, primarily because I was tired of being around so many people who found comfort in failure. Other people might have viewed my ditching an education from NYU as catastrophic for my future, but the last time I checked, NYU didn't have a class for being a pop recording artist as big as the late, great Prince. (The moment I met George Michael in London was the moment I was going into a movie theater in Leicester Square to see Prince's *Purple Rain*. What an inspirational day, I'd say.) Before the plane touched down at Heathrow, I knew I wanted to be a pop star—not pretend to be one, but really take a chance to *live* as one (to me, the definition of stardom was to be able to create, sing and perform for a living—it wasn't only having the opportunity to have a hoard of money); and I knew I had something that was worthy enough for the category. That was my big dream, and I decided to embark on a trip across the pond to try my best to make it all come true.

I was ready for the opportunity and didn't put up any psychological roadblocks to sabotage myself. And I got the deal, the record, the tour, and the fans (all five of them!). Mission accomplished. Even though I left music, I didn't exit through the back door solely because I was afraid to dream about being successful in it. With an inner voice as loud as the Mormon Tabernacle Choir, I had no other choice but to find the courage to leave music, which was as bold as choosing to dive into it in the first place. Trust me, you probably have never heard of me before this book, but as I hinted in the Intro, if you do a little Googling, you'll find all that "Larry Loeber" recorded—when I was thirty-two years younger.

#Before your plane takes off, dream big.

My hope for you is as follows:

If you are lucky enough to live past eighty, I want you to sit in that rocking chair with a smile, satisfied that you gave it your all, not wondering, "What if?" To get you started, here's my first **"TAKE-A-QUIZ"** to make sure you're ready to embark on the road to your big dream:

1. **What's your strategy to make your dream come true?** Every dream comes from somewhere, and I can promise you there were many incarnations of the Empire State Building before it looked as grand as it does. Like the building, every goal starts with a plan to build it. The foundation for your dream will come, if you're willing to take the time to research and learn about your specialty or your market and are fully prepared before you take the educated risk you need to let your imagination fly. Make your dream a reality—not simply stuck in the fantasy of a reality TV show!

2. **Are you afraid to take the first step?** Just like a diet of food, a diet of success is the hardest when you just start out...because your negative mind plays tricks on you. Have the courage to dive deeply into a pool of success through imagining you're there, even before you

start. OK. If you're a scaredy cat, dip your toe in and start small...but *start*!

3. **Are you caught up in negative chatter?** Remember, it takes as much energy to work with the negative as it does to work with upbeat people who gravitate towards each other and don't feel weird if someone else succeeds. No man is an island. Reach out and find *good people* to hobnob with. If possible, find that one person who can be your ally of strength and support, and once you feel comfortable, expand your network. Choose a trusted confidant or band of supporters who you know will give you honest advice. Take a close friend or loved one out for coffee, and share your secret passion. Give them your spiel, and watch them listen. Work the idea out and tighten it up, so that when it's time to share it to the world, you will be ready.

4. **Do you lack confidence in your dream?** Before you self-edit, listen to your own pitch out loud to make sure it's true to the dream you have put in place. If you're locked in a moment of your life where you just can't take a risk because you're worried what Aunt Bertha will think, remember: at this stage of her life, Auntie is most likely only capable of asking you to change her bedpan... she doesn't know anything about your dreams, frankly... let alone hers. Be selfish (not greedy): It's time for your dream and your life—not hers.

5. **Is your dream really your nightmare?** Don't sugarcoat a nightmare into a dream—or if your dream

has gone sour, have the courage to admit it's over, and move on. If you're not meant to play a concerto with an orchestra, forget it. If your version of a recording career ain't happening, look at it realistically and take emotional inventory. Maybe you're really not good enough. Or maybe this dream really *isn't* what you want. If it is truly your dream, but no one else agrees with your choice, ask yourself whether you've given it your all, and whether it's worth continuing or moving on. No one, including you, should stay at a party when it's over! But the saying "It's not over 'till it's over" really means that. Give it your all before packing it in.

If it weren't for dreams, there would be no inventions for heat, light, or shelter, let alone all the gadgets that keep our world running. If it weren't for dreams, we would not be able to drink clean water; we wouldn't believe we could live in a world without war or that we all deserve to love each other beyond our race, creed, sexual orientation, and color. If it weren't for dreams, we would not believe we could treat each other with respect and get ahead in our lives without stepping on others. If any or all of these dreams flirt with your dossier, I encourage you to add more line items like this to your dare-to-do list. Remember—without apology—be brave! You have the ability to renegotiate your wish list at any time without judgment so that your fortunes will read in the "now," not in the "what if?" Most importantly, you have the ability to tear down your personal walls of insecurity and fear, and get out of your own way. You have the ability to be your worst enemy...and your best friend. Give yourself a hug, and go for it!

Step Two:

Make a Good First Impression

Making a good first impression is the key that opens up the winning personality inside you. When we see adults still squirming at the idea of meeting new people at a party, it brings us all back to meeting our fellow kindergarten class for the first time. Awkward!

It's time to learn how to make a good impression. Remember, I was that little kid who sounded like a squeaky girl on the phone—imagine how confident I was in those days, if you had met me? *EEK!* I was a walking disaster with a big butt; however, after exhausting my exhaustion of feeling so painfully shy every time I picked up the phone or walked into a room, I realized that once I mastered a grand entrance, it was the ticket for me to get out of my own way and do my thing. In this step, you'll see how to make a first impression and how to unravel one, which is equally as important when dealing with others on all different levels.

As far as the job environment goes, it's important to be conscious of how you're perceived by your colleagues.

Mary was a super-smart lady. All of her degrees and her know-how did not negate the fact she had an odor problem, and according to colleagues, she was known as "Miss Piggypen." The more perfume Mary wore, and the more Manolos she scuffed around the office, her smell was always the first impression everyone seemed to have of her. Paul, the HR person, took the responsibility to have a heart-to-heart with Mary, because the poor girl was turning into a butt of all jokes, rather than praised for a superb job well done. After a personal chat with Mary—Paul had asked whether she would like to have a consultation with the company's medical office— Mary admitted to knowing about the odor problem, but thought it had dissipated. It seems as if her diet played a big part in her medical predicament, and with a certain tweak of foods and supplements, Mary turned her ailment around in a few weeks.

**#It's better to tell a person they have
toilet paper dragging from their shoe
than let them wipe up the floor with jokes told about them.**

Making a first impression in your personal life is as important as it is in the workplace. Have you heard the phrase, "reading" people? It's when you look someone up and down and give a smirk of approval or dissatisfaction. Who on Earth are we to judge others strictly by what they look like, what they sound like, and what they're wearing? When you only judge a book by its cover, you're doing yourself a disservice because, frankly, you look insecure, small-minded, and stupid. Dealing with people on the surface impedes your body language, your tone, and your overall actions and reactions. With the good old smartphone, people have developed these fake alter egos that forbid others from understanding just who they really are, other than a false impression. Just look at all the dating apps. When it comes to unravelling the layers of online dating, many are so afraid of being tricked or duped, it seems to be a rarity when people tell their real age or even show a recent photo. Unless you have absolutely no intention of meeting anyone through online dating, do you really think that someone you meet can't tell that you've gained eighty-five pounds since the picture you posted on the Internet? C'mon, people! Have confidence in who you are, no matter how you look.

#Lying about who you are is lying to yourself.

And then there are those who aren't lying to anyone, but choosing to keep their life a big secret.

Remember that awesome game show host, Chuck Barris, who fronted *The Gong Show* and created *The Dating Game* and *The Newlywed Game*? Apparently while he was busy entertaining us, he was living a double life, working for the CIA as an assassin in the 1960s and the 1970s. Talking about starring in your own version of Dr. Jekyll and Mr. Hyde!

For those of us who aren't spies or terrorists looking to extort money from others, my vote would be for everyone to be honest and up front with those who share a similar quest— for example, stepping up to the plate when looking for a perfect date, or stepping away if you're not quite the perfect candidate for a job with specific responsibilities. That doesn't mean that you have to wear your heart on your sleeve in every circumstance; however, once you're known as someone who is genuine, people will look up to you and trust you.

Walking into a room and proclaiming who you are is as if you're promoting your personality on a billboard. Entering in a conversation with someone who you've just met for the first time is like playing a game of ping-pong: lobbing the convo back and forth (so as not to crash into the net), but playing the game long enough where you'll know who's going to come out on top. Will you talk so long that you wear out your welcome, or will you act as intriguing as Chuck Barris and mysteriously excuse yourself from the chatter?

During my recording days in London, I remember coming to the conclusion that even though the Brits speak English, we definitely *do not* speak the same language—making the art of developing impressions of each other very complicated. Imagine being in a recording studio, in the middle of going through a jam session, when you see your techno-programmer write on a paper that he "quits"—and then he walks out, never to be seen again. Imagine the inner hell that that musician must've gone through to get to the point where he couldn't simply look the band in the eye and say, "I'm sorry, this isn't working out; today will be my last day."

I bet that if you stop and think about your life, and if you make a point to share a healthy dose of honesty and transparency with people, it will ultimately bring you rewards (and spare you heartaches and headaches). When you take the time and effort to go beyond the small talk, you'll make more meaningful connections—as opposed to conversing with them as if you're an iTunes recording on "repeat." And when you sit back and take the temperature of the people you are gradually getting to know (or, more accurately, the people you *think* you know), you'll be able to decide whether a person is someone you want to keep in your fold or toss to the curb.

Just about everyone has a story of being fooled by a first impression. Here are a few of mine....

...During my teenage years, I made at least two really stupid mistakes. First off, I was taken by a couple of cons who were kings of small talk: one who asked me to hold a heavy package as he described to me the contents inside. I was so interested in the "stereo equipment" that I forgot to actually open up the box before I gave this dude two hundred dollars—only to discover this was a box of magazines. Then, there was the time a man walked down Tenth Street (between Fifth and Sixth Avenue— the block I lived on at the time), in NYC and asked if I had forty bucks to help him get home upstate because he had lost his wallet. I gave him the money because I was so moved by his story. Why did I see both of them in the neighborhood the next day—working his same routine? Answer: I saw these crooks as friends first, instead of looking at them for face value.

Here's a totally different example that changed my life forever, and the one that I would describe as the epitome of my mother's spirit.

Growing up, my parents hired a live-in housekeeper (now known as a nanny) named Monica. Though a hard worker, Monica always found the time to talk and listen to me. In some ways, Monica filled the void I had as an only child, and really was like an aunt or a big sister to me. So I was sad to hear Monica crying every night because, unbeknownst to me and my parents, she desperately missed her little girl Dawn back in Trinidad. When we all learned that Monica's mission in America was to make a solid living in order to pay for Dawn's schooling, clothing, food—you name it—we started to look beyond our first impression of her. More than just a housekeeper, it was clear that Monica was a great mother, who desperately missed her daughter with all her heart and soul, and who had a zest for giving Dawn the life she never had.

That mind shift about Monica really affected my mom, who morphed from the woman who overprotected me, to Elayne Atlas Loeber Papadopoulos, a dynamo who would not take anyone's crap since her divorce from my biological dad. I wondered why my mom was so interested in learning more and more about Dawn. Elayne kept asking Monica questions about her daughter's age, height, weight, shoe size, address— pressing her for way too much information that employers and housekeepers don't typically chat about.

As for Monica, if she had died while mopping our floors with her tears, at the time her "hashtag takeaway" memorial might have read something like this:

#At first glance, she was a woman surrounded by sadness, but supported by will.

Because the real Monica melted before our eyes, Mom didn't want Monica to feel sad any longer.

Along with Dawn's personal stats, Monica gave Elayne her home address in Trinidad because mom wanted to send Dawn a care package of clothes, shoes, and goodies she thought the little girl would enjoy. But sending a gift to Dawn was only the beginning. It was a few weeks later when my mom surprised Monica (and us all), by bringing Dawn up to Jersey for a surprise visit! Elayne worked out the trip with one of Monica's sisters and met the little girl at the airport. The "vacation" lasted until little Dawn (who I first met at six years old) GRADUATED from my high school! That's right, Monica and Dawn lived with us, and my mom made sure Dawn had the education she deserved.

#A good deed makes a lasting impression.

Not only was I excited to have a little "sister" (who had such a tiny wrist—she was like a porcelain doll), but at that moment, I saw how the power of making a solid impression influenced people. At first glance, you would have thought my mom spent more time at the beauty parlor fluffing herself than helping her housekeeper find a way to bring her daughter from Trinidad to America. And that's how a first impression can fool you.

#Never judge a book by its cover.

#Never think a beautiful woman isn't a smart tigress ready to change the world.

Here's another incident where an authentic first impression changed the course of my life and my mom's. During a summer vacation way back in the 70s, my mom took me on a cruise and thought I had fallen overboard. Mom launched a hunt for me: she gathered all of the crew and the captain, and went screaming "Larry, Larry, Larry!" throughout the vessel, including the ship's movie theater, which is where I was—watching a flick. Well, the sound of hearing my first name shouted like that brought back memories of hearing it coupled with Miss Vancheri again—debilitating. Instead of revealing myself, in panic, I slid under the theater seats and hid. Minutes later, I walked out of the show and saw my mom crying profusely, surrounded by the captain and crew, who didn't know what to do with a woman who had, it seemed, just lost her son. When she saw me, it was like the "Dawn/Monica" reunion moment. Shortly thereafter, just as magically, the captain on that ship became my stepdad.

#You never know when a first impression leads to true love.

**#Never underestimate those around you
who are simply *listening*.**

When my stepdad, Captain Anthony George Papadopoulos, saw the way my mother cared for me, he told me that that was the moment he fell in love with Elayne. My mom was fourteen years older than him, but her strength, her brains, her beauty, and her first impression made them undeniable soulmates until Elayne's death in 2005.

Now a solid and upbeat seventysomething (Tony is only fifteen years older than I), the first impression you get of my stepdad might not be as passionate as his life reveals. When you see Tony walking down the street, you would not know he piloted thousands of American tourists to the Caribbean as captain of some of the biggest cruise ships of the day. You would not know he was a captain of the Merchant Marine, manning vessels transporting tanks and missiles in the Gulf War, and you would

definitely not know he led his ship fighting off pirates to save
the crew and the vessel. When you see Tony walking now with
his dear companion June, you would never know that she and
her late husband built a huge nationally-acclaimed food empire
either. I promise you that *everyone* has an amazing story, and
you're simply not going to know all the chapters at first glance.

What do you think are people's first impressions of you?

Do you think you will be known as thoughtful, impressive, shy,
eager, charitable...or a time bomb ready to implode? Will you
be known as a backstabber? Without any hype, what is your
real deal that people will remember you for? You probably
know better than anyone else. Not all of us will have streets,
schools, or bridges named after us—but many people are heroes
like Mother Teresa: quiet giants who show their greatness by
doing good deeds for others. I know we all want to fit in, but:

#The first person we have to fit in for is ourselves.

Before you go to your next outing, job interview, or blind date,
here's your next **"TAKE-A-QUIZ"** to help you get out of your
own way and enjoy the experience at hand:

1. **How do strangers perceive you?** If you're sitting
   at the party, in the corner with a sourpuss face on, I can
   guarantee people will think you're an ass—when most
   likely you're scared shitless. After all these years on the
   planet, do you really want to have so much anxiety about
   meeting new people? C'mon, take a breath and shake
   up your persona. Crack a smile. Chances are you'll get
   one back. If you don't, not to worry. The more you put

yourself out there, the more you'll forget the people who aren't friendly. And if you are really trying your best and still can't go up to someone and break the ice, perhaps you need to see a therapist and work out your issues of low self esteem. No Joke.

2. **What's your first "read" on a person? Looks?** Remember, if you're only looking at face value, keep in mind that looks can be deceiving. Someone who seems really put together might be miserable, or awful to deal with...and someone who looks shabby might be a diamond in the rough. Remember: Mary was known as "Miss Piggypen," but after she solved her health issues, people noticed her brilliance.

3. **Are you comfortable with small talk?** If the answer is not good at all, here's the secret: A chitchat with a stranger is like a dance. Introduce, then listen, then reply. Remember the key to small talk is to pull an interesting sound bite out of a conversation and then expand on it from there. The more you ask and show your interest in someone, the more flattered and invested they'll be in the conversation. And who knows? Outa this convo, you just might meet your future boss, business partner, BFF, or soulmate.

4. **How do you rate your handshake?** A handshake is a key into someone's personality. If you have a wimpy, clammy handshake, most people will take you for weak. If you're in doubt as to whether your handshake exudes confidence, ask a friend to analyze your shake with you.

If you still can't get rid of the wet palms, a doctor might actually help stop the problem with Botox.

5. **Where's your focus?** When you're meeting people for the first time, focus on *them*. It's so frustrating to be having a conversation with someone and they're looking elsewhere. If you look someone in the eye, you're subconsciously saying to them, "I think you're worth focusing on." If you still can't get their attention, they might not be worth spending time with.

Giving a good first impression clears the path for conversation, and allows others to gravitate to you—even employers. People want to be around a winning personality—and what better way to get the party started then with a smile, a hello, a strong show of interest, and a healthy dose of confidence? If you put yourself out there, you definitely will get something back in return—and if you come off as a welcoming person, the chances are your return on your time invested will be well worth it.

Step Three:

Find Perfection in Imperfection

Attention, anyone who desperately wants to be perfect—in looks, in career, in love, in life: if that's you, respectfully, take a major step out of your own way, because the idea of being perfect is debilitating and unachievable. You might be asking why the hell am I adding a tip about celebrating flaws in your life as a way to succeed? As anyone who knows anything about America, we're not only the supposed land of the free and home of the brave; we're a celebrity-watching, image-conscious, weight-obsessed, and brainiac-focused nation whose marketers out there seem to think the world is run by kids—that is, those people who don't work—and whose parents, the ones who pay their bills, are irrelvant. I never understood why marketers dismiss those who hold onto the purse strings in favor of those with youth and beauty. That's why it's only apropos to include a step focusing primarily on how everyday people like me and you should give ourselves a break when we think we're imperfect—not aspire to be like The Friggen' Joneses.

I'm practically doubled over with herniated laughter at the idea we're all clamoring to look twenty-six again, because frankly— and absolutely no disrespect to the Millennials out there—my twenties were so painful (you remember my life merry-go-round in the Intro?), it was as if I was stuck in the agitation cycle of a washing machine—unable to give myself a full rinse. Some days I wish I was Japanese, a culture where young people respect the elderly, not like here in America, where, according to the Ten O'Clock News, teenagers seem to be beating up old people at the ATM machine (with hidden cameras rolling) for grandma's measly seventy-five bucks. It's so weird to think that American marketers zero in on the tweenies, the teenies, and the ones who should barely wear bikinis, since according to the most recent US Census Bureau count, there are nearly forty-five million Americans sixty-five and older. The Bureau predicts that in 2060 there will be over ninety-eight million. As we plump, tighten, smooth out, and freeze, what the hell is everyone worried about? Getting old should be a positive fact of life. (Duh, the only alternative is a nail in your coffin!) Let's put the scalpels down for a moment, kick off our shoes, pull the fake eyelashes off, and put our teeth in a glass of water, shall we?

Let's continue this mini-rant with the idea of physical perfection, which in America (and other cultures) seems to be the number one ticket to success, love, money—you name it. Being gorgeous, thin, and muscular is a stairway to stardom. As you may recall, I'm from Jersey, but I'm not sure what was going on with every parent and teenager in South Orange (my hometown) in the 1960s, which was probably the first decade when parents were creating "little monsters of perfection." It seemed as if it was a rite of passage for many of my ilk to get a nose job for their Bar or Bat Mitzvah—basically to look WASPier, I guess. My friends tell me I'm the original JLo because I have the biggest ass—and had the frizziest Afro, uh, Jewfro—this side of the Mississippi. And from years and years of self-assessment and a few good ones focusing on therapy, I'm told that I have fairly nice eyes, nice cheekbones (when I'm on the thin side), naturally appropriately plumped lips, and a nice nose. This is no joke: friends would practically drag me to their nose doctors to use me as a nostril model as they begged their plastic surgeons to try and replicate my schnozolla. Now

I'm looking at my schnoz as I write about it, and I can see it being a nice set of two holes and a bridge, before the "catastrophy." That's right: in the 80s, my cat, Gabriel, scratched the left side of my nostril, forcing me to get over twelve stitches right where the left side flares out. So this old nose isn't going on to appear on HDTV anytime soon!

In all truth, who really needs a perfect honker, anyway? (Frankly, I would rather have had higher SAT scores than a nice nose.) In retrospect, where would the entertainment world be without the ski-sloped nostrils of the great Barbra Streisand? Here's a woman who could have chopped off her breathers, but she chose to keep herself "herself," whom many (including me) believe is pure perfection. (Please tell me you know who Babs is?!)

It's so sad to think that those with an imperfect nose, imperfect lips, or even imperfect private parts, believe that their "flaws" will somehow *not* get them an audition on the latest *Baywatch* sequel. On the other hand, it's a tragedy that our greatest drama schools don't tell its prospective thespians (and parents footing the tuition) that the business is not only about being talented. It's about looks too.

#Looking perfect is in the eyes of the beholder.

#If you want to be in showbiz, have a backup plan just in case your curtain isn't going up.

Why is America obsessed with hair, and why didn't I keep mine? (Supposedly, when it comes to hair, you follow the gene pattern of your mother. FYI, my grandfather on my mother's side had a full head of it. Go figure.) I was practically the poster child for hair transplant surgery. In the early 80s, I remember going to a fancy hair-plug doctor on Fifth Avenue in NYC (I was so excited to see former *Cosmo* editor-in-chief Helen Gurley Brown sitting in the waiting room—what the hell was she doing there?) A week or two after that star sighting, I also remember walking out of the same doc's office fresh from the inpatient hair procedure with a head that looked like hamburger meat, wrapped in bandages like Liz Taylor in *Ash Wednesday*. You see, in those days, fancy doctors would punch out a patient's hair follicles from their own donor sites in clumps; in my opinion, all the guys who went through this procedure looked awful. Those hairy wefts went from point A (the side and back of the scalp) to point B (the front where most hairlines were receding). What the snotty doc didn't tell me when I got it done is that the success is only as good as the amount of donor sites you can provide to the bare ones...it was as if you were robbing your own Peter to pay Paul! (No Mary in sight, that's for sure.) And sadly, I didn't have enough hairy inventory to fill in the balding spots. So my fantasy of my Jewfro blowing back in the wind once again was lost in translation.

Although I didn't inherit a wealth of hair, I did inherit the fat gene. I have gained and lost sixty pounds probably sixty times already. If I hear another physician tell me that's unhealthy, I'm going to wrap them in bacon and serve them up as hors d'oeuvres at an Overeaters Anonymous meeting.

#When you're looking for perfection, don't forget to read the small print.

**#What's considered perfect today
isn't necessarily tomorrow.**

**#I might be known as the original "Justin,"
but my last name will never be Timberlake.**

Let's face it, people: we are not perfect. We are all beautiful, unique specimens—as if our bodies were a thumbprint—only special to us and no one else. Again, anyone who you think is perfect is telling a lie or hiding a deep secret. For years, I worked so hard to be the epitome of perfection, but it was exhausting and blew up in my face—nostrils and all—and a roadblock that, for years, kept me from getting out of my own way. Think about it. If everyone had a cute little button nose, a body with just the right amount of curves, and hair flowing farer and wider than Rapunzel, how could anyone stand out from the crowd? That's why I truly believe:

#There is perfection in imperfection.

As soon as we believe that our character flaws and physical impurities are our strengths, it *will* get us a part in *Baywatch: Real People Exposed!!* or attract the "perfect" Mr. or Ms. Right for you.

So what if you have tree trunk ankles? Wear slacks if that bothers you.

So what if you have a muffin top? Go on a diet or get some Spanx—they also come in a men's tee.

If you have big ears, and you're not bald, hide them by growing your hair over them.

Big here, too small there, not enough here and there; it's all bull-doody. We are fed this crap because it keeps the beauty business in business.

#Beauty is in the eyes of your plastic surgeon.

What do you hate about yourself?

I can promise you (unless a dermatologist gives you a valid medical reason to remove it) that mole on your cheek is not hideous. Did you ever notice that if you dye your hair or grow a beard, people who you haven't seen in a while will say, "What is it about you that's different?" I'm sorry to burst your bubble, but people aren't so engrossed by you that they take a test about every look and every glance you make. No one cares, because everyone is focused on themselves. Get over yourself and live your life uniquely, without apology. Your deep, cracking voice and your bodacious booty might not be for everyone, but it only takes one person to take notice.

#What you see as flaws in yourself aren't "secrets revealed" to others.

If all people had the same svelte physique, there would never have been a Marilyn Monroe. If all people had the same speaking voices, there would never have been a Walter Cronkite or a James Earl Jones. If all people cracked the same jokes, there would never have been a Joan Rivers.

# # #

Let's move onto the notion of being perfect in your career. In business, if everyone were perfect, our workdays would be so boring. If every job candidate walked into an interview like they were a brand-new ping-pong ball, how the hell would the powers that be know who to hire? Who wants to emulate a robotsports equipment, anyway? Trust me, if our culture could save a buck hiring a robot to do our jobs, most of us would be canned. However, if anyone saw the 2016 movie *Passengers* (with Jennifer Lawrence, Chris Pratt, and stupendous special effects), you will recall the "Arthur" character (and even the ship) wasn't what it all seemed. Talk about smoke and mirrors, and robots gone wild!

I remember distinctly when one of my fave employees of all time, Udan, sent me a cover letter practically begging me to see him because even though he wasn't "the perfect" candidate, he passionately felt he was the right one because he brought his own unique "brand" to the table. (Good pitch, Udan!) Here he was living the American Dream—coming from one country to sleep on his sister's couch to help him find the "perfect" opportunity in work—so that he could get off his butt and make a life for himself, and make a difference for others.

At first, Udan was right—he wasn't the perfect candidate. What he lacked in traditional skills, he made up for it with the power of the English language. How "perfect"

GET OUT OF YOUR OWN WAY GUIDE TO LIFE

for an employer in communications to hire someone who knew how to speak, to write, to express his innermost feelings with an endearing heart and soul that didn't turn you off because of some sort of naïveté?

# # #

As passionate as Udan was, Marnie was a "raw talent" to say the least. For someone like me who considers himself a cheerleader for an entry-level staffer, I love helping those who come in exuding a sense of purpose. While the other staffers were busy "playing by the rules," Marnie was a firecracker. The traits most people might have frowned upon when dealing with Marnie were the very things that made me consider her a rising star. You see, people spend thousands and thousands of dollars to learn the passion and the perseverance that Marnie embraced naturally. To me, she had no weaknesses—all strengths— she was simply a victim of her youth, who desperately needed training. In the middle of her natural drama, Marnie didn't realize that she was so polite and humble (another amazing trait to have when working with people), she was like a sponge sopping up Goldenseal Tea. If Marnie was interested in learning, I was ready and willing to help her.

#Become an expert in the traits that come naturally to you.

So, we've touched upon beauty and career, what's left when it comes to the notion of perfection? I could not write a book like this without including a few paragraphs about love. Sadly, I look around and see many of my straight friends separated or divorced. Why? Unanimously, my friends tell me there was so much pressure to live in a "perfect" marriage, that the idea of communing with someone they truly loved, versus one who could compete in the one-up Olympics with The Friggen' Joneses, was unattainable. The pressure from family and friends to join in on the "married couples" club was so intense for many of my friends; it's so sad to think that many of them have broken up.

On the other end of the spectrum, I'm not quite sure why *all* of my gay married friends have been together for decades? Could it have anything to do with the fact there really wasn't an expectation or pressure from anyone to get married to the same sex? Expectations, societal as well as personal, distract us from what we want and get in the way of what we truly feel.

> After twenty years of living together, Jim and Peter decided they wanted to get married. Not that they needed to give off an aura of perfection—they were desperately afraid that the government was going to take away their rights to be with each other if one of them became ill. Can you imagine living with someone for decades and being denied rights to see them in their last days? Talk about a fucking imperfect and heartless system we live in.

I don't know if you realize it, but when it comes to love, gay men and straight women share the same challenges—both of these demographics are tossed away by their culture when they've reached a certain age. (Oh, BTW: I'm gay, and there's more about this aspect of my life story later in the book. Spoiler alert! Anyway...). Is there more respect in Japan for older gay people? If so, sayonara people—I'm catching the next JAL flight to Tokyo, the land where they treat old geezers like gold!

Seriously, I'm so disappointed to learn that in this day and age, older people in general feel they need to lie about their age in order to compete in the workplace, and appear attractive to others. At this point, I'm so lucky to even be alive, and have the experience and opportunities I've had, I can't believe anyone would dismiss that as a negative.

My hope in this world is we all take a breath and celebrate what we have to offer, not what we compare to. Some people are great mathematicians, but are horrible when it comes to street smarts. Some people who drop out of college, make great personalities. Has anyone heard of Mark Zuckerberg, Ellen DeGeneres, Oprah, Lady Gaga, John Lennon or Steve Jobs?

Think of a world with Oprah Winfrey as President of the United States. Whatever you think of her as a TV personality, you know she's always trying to strive for a sense of authenticity, serenity and perfection. In my opinion, there is no one more *thoughtful* in the public eye than Oprah, don't you think? How could anyone *not* vote for someone whose pride and joy these days is appearing on a show called *Super Soul Sunday*? It might not be on a major network and it might not have the highest ratings, but it is perfect in its focused intimacy.

#If Oprah was President, we would be living in harmony and the world would be preserved for our children.

As you think about and ponder the idea of Oprah running for office, let's **"TAKE-A-QUIZ"** to make sure you get my drift that imperfection is pure perfection for yourself. Here goes:

1. **Are you obsessed with your flaws?** Remember Barbra Streisand's choice to keep her honker as is, which literally helped to make her millions? We all have physical flaws. So maybe you have thin lips or close-set eyes or protruding ears. Embrace whatever makes you look imperfect as perfectly, uniquely *you*. Find a way to turn your flaws into your trademark.

2. **Are you exhausted by trying to be perfect at all times?** Perfection implies that there is no such thing as evolution. After all, a stone statue doesn't move.... Do you really want to be constantly hard as a rock, even outside of the bedroom? (Joke.) Seriously, give yourself a break and let yourself live in the extraordinary skin you are living in. I don't know about you, but Siri is one imperfect chick and as dumb as a doornail. Every time I ask her to dial my work number, that dipsy doodle has the nerve to say she doesn't know who I am. Really, Siri?

3. **Are you focused on "them" instead of celebrating "you?"** There will always be a Bieber, a Grande, a Crawford, a Drake, and a Rihanna. Someone will always

look better, sound better, swagger more smoothly...but I guarantee that when you open your eyes and crack the smile you were born with, you too will be ready for your close-up.

4. **Do you go into a deep depression when you fail a test or lose a competition?** Coming from a person who got a 390 (Math score) and a 420 (English score) on his SATs, I'm telling you: put your depression to bed. If your parents wanted you to be an attorney (and you're not into it), or you've spent a lifetime in a career you hate just to fit in with The Friggen' Joneses, let it go; finally, develop the traits you were born with. If the notion of initially dropping out didn't hurt President-elect Oprah (OK, so I want to be her campaign manager, people!), it certainly won't hurt you. Love yourself.

5. **Do you have fear of being dismissed because you're growing older?** Newsflash! Every healthy and unhealthy person is growing older. Even the ones who wear thongs and Speedos. Celebrate your life—as old or as you as you may be—and take note that you've done something right so far because you're still here.

Even our picture-perfect icons aren't perfect. Look at Whitney Houston and Robin Williams. Get it? But the beauty within is the beauty that a beholder will see...if you allow them access into your heart and soul. If the woman in da Vinci's *Mona Lisa* and the man who modeled Michelangelo's *David* were living in Beverly Hills circa 2017, the pressure to be forever beautiful would be enormous: she would have already had rhinoplasty, he would have had a penis enlargement. (How sad.) Even though both are celebrated for their perfection, both would be as dumb as marble and paint because that is really what they're made of. As for yourself, dig deeper. I know you'll hit gold.

Step Four:

Know Your Sh*t!

OMG, it's time for us to take more inventory of ourselves. Hmmm. Are you really ready? Many of us lack the time to focus, especially if we know subconsciously that what we need to home in on is a bit painful. For a lot of us, it's easier to focus on someone else's crap than it is for us to work through our own. When life's problems are coming at you like a freight train, it's only natural to freeze the emotion and bury it, trust me. But if a feeling is like an ice cube, it doesn't simply melt and turn into water. As time ticks on, your frozen emotions are still the same festering feelings—not very useful if you're desperately trying to get out from under your emotional rollercoaster that is stuck at the top of the ride. Although we think we know our sh*t, c'mon now, many of us don't have a clue. Is that you?

#Be honest.

Some of us lack "self," which blocks our emotional roadway from moving forward—from evolving. Think about this: what if you nay-sayers out there stopped being jaded, got rid of your baggage, threw it out the window, and walked into life with a clean slate and a smile on your face?

I'm willing to offer you a clean slate, if you take this free self-assessment.

10 Signs You Might Not Know Your Sh*t!:

1. You don't think a potential recruiter will find the amateur porno video you posted on the Internet six years ago.

2. Your resume is half made-up, and the other half is cut-and-pasted from another person's LinkedIn.

3. You have a major presentation you should be preparing for, but you're playing World of Warcraft.

4. You are so bored at work, you can't be bothered to read the urgent memo your boss sent you.

5. Your bills are piling up, and even though you've got the money in the bank to pay them, you couldn't care less if you're late or not.

6. Your puppy needs to pee-pee and you're more focused on texting your new love interest.

7. You dismissed the 911 emergency call when the grandparent who raised you was rushed to the hospital.

8. You think you're fat at a size zero.

9. You forget to cash your twenty thousand dollars in lottery winnings.

10. After two years, you haven't come to grips that your best friend committing suicide.

In order to figure out your strategy for life—to work out your sh*t, you have to stop worrying about The Friggen' Joneses and "come to Jesus" (or your chosen higher authority) as you really are, fully exposed. You can't hide behind your Prada bag and Air Jordans any longer. We all have a threshold when our bodies say, "Keep pushing forward because you are a super-person" or, "Stop, because you can't go any further."

That's why:

#You really have to know your sh*t in order to get out of your own way and be comfortable in your own skin.

Whether you know it or not, I truly believe that most of us, you and me included, want to do the best we can because we're put on the planet for a purpose. To fulfill that purpose, we need to know our capabilities. Some people are capable of jumping out of an airplane, some can make a mean apple pie—whatever it is, filling your capacity tank with what you know (and don't know) about yourself helps you embark on the road of personal enlightenment.

My favorite person of all times, Demetra, was a rising Broadway superstar. If this girl stayed home for a week, it would be a miracle. Traveling here, traveling there, Demi (as we called her) knew her sh*t more than anyone I knew. She came from humble beginnings, had absolutely no support from her family, basically taught herself to dance, and pulled it all together to land some of the most important Broadway shows of our century. Hell, when she was called to fill in for the role of Evita in Paris, she fucking learned the French score in a week! To say that Demi had the capacity for standing on the stage and commanding attention was an understatement.

After years and years of traveling, Demi began losing steam and caring less and less about the showbiz thing. You would be tired too if you performed in over twenty-one countries in a decade. What an amazing experience to see the world through the eyes of theater; however, now it was time for Demi to come home.

#When you know the curtain has come down, exit, stage left.

When Demi came back to the States, she was welcomed by an invalid uncle and debt from here to eternity, because Demi's ex-boyfriend-turned-friend, Joe, was a procrastinator and never paid the bills for her on time— and we all know what happens when you forget to pay the mortgage and car payments.

With ten years of traveling under her belt, Demi had nothing to show for it because she was a spendaholic. Instead of panicking (at this point she understood that panic doesn't solve problems), she took a breath and admitted she could not change the past—she needed to change her future. It was time for Demi to find a quiet opportunity—to make a living where her adrenaline wasn't always pumping. What did Demi do? She took a clerk job at the local town hall in upstate New York.

At first, I didn't understand how a diva who sang the shit out of an Andrew Lloyd Weber score could now punch in at 9:00 am and punch out at the end of the day. The fact is, it doesn't matter what I understood or didn't—I wasn't paying her bills. It was what Demi needed to do. Even though she chose to spend her next "act" in the mundane, she was able to finally get herself out of debt, and even save money for a down payment on a townhouse!

**#If you're not paying your friend's bills,
you have no right to tell them how they spend their money.**

Whether they enlightened or frustrated me, Demi's choices pushed me to see her as a true survivor, capable of making decisions authentically because the only person she had to please and live up to was herself.

**#It bears repeating:
you are NOT here to live like The Friggen' Joneses.**

You've heard the cliché that we come into and leave the world alone? If Demi's story can be a source of inspiration for you, understand that she made a personal pact with herself that she wouldn't be rolling up in an Access-a-Ride somewhere, whether at sixty or ninety, wondering what it would have been like if she didn't own her own home and had never overcome debt. As for your own personal contract, you can fill in the blank.

To make this super-easy for you to grasp, let's use me as the guinea pig to see if I know my sh*t. I'll demonstrate how the hashtags dotted throughout this book can really mean something, especially if you tailor-make your own fortune cookie fortunes. And don't forget: as you learn how to get out of your own way, evolve, and grow, your hashtags can keep on changing based on where you are in your life.

So let's just see if I know my own sh*t.

About yours truly, friends and family would say:

#Great survivor and self-made entrepreneur.

#Loyal.

#He will take the shirt off his back
and give you his last crumb.

#Sooo funny!

#Is he really an old fuckin' geezer? Seems like he's 38–42.

#When he sets his mind to do something,
he does it surprisingly well.

#Idiot savant in real estate.

#A worrywart.
He over-analyzes things to the point of exhaustion.

#He dates down.

#He's moody, a bit whiney, and at times a hypochondriac.

**#Uses food as a crutch
and eats way too many sweets and carbs.**

**#When it's time to go "no carbs,"
he embraces it cold turkey.**

#Wears his emotions on his sleeve.

**#Has trust issues. Could it be because
his late biological father's mistress-turned-second-wife
screwed him out of his inheritance?**

Didn't that last hashtag sound angry? You're damn straight—
we'll go into that a little more at the end of this book. So, if
you're in a predicament where the hashtag is destined for
a therapy session (and you don't have the funds or energy
to work it out with a professional counselor), here's what
I do: grab a big-ass pillow and beat it until it flattens like a
pancake. Trust me when I tell you that hitting a pillow is very
therapeutic. (Note: if you are big and strong, buy a manmade
one so that feathers don't fly all over the place.)

OK, back to my self-assessment. Now, staffers would say:

#He gave me a chance.

**#He works his ass off for the business
and expects the staff to rise to the occasion too.**

#He believes in diversity.

#Sometimes forgets that he already delegated something.

#Isn't always a great manager. Is he bipolar?!

#Generous.

#At times, lacks patience.

#Can be the biggest prick on the face of the planet.

#He is so annoying...won't let up if something isn't right.

**#If he tells me about his days as a
disco recording artist again, I'm going to throw up.**

**#He has a very high bottom line
and encourages me to be the best I can be.**

#He has a low tolerance for bullshit.

**#He has given me the
training I need in my job to be a success.**

#He is thoughtful.

#He never forgets to pay us.

Are you getting my drift now? So, I'm not proud of exposing my "inner prick" of a personality, but I am proud of being loyal. Perhaps, because I admit to being imperfect, the good traits balance out the bad ones?

After it's all said and done, here's what I would say
about myself:

#I am all of the hashtags above.

**#I have a backstory running in my head
faster than I speak. Undiagnosed ADHD. Frustrating.**

**#When life gets stressful, I turn my brain into a punch list
and tick off each line item.**

#I don't know how to totally relax.

#Fear of losing business drives me.

#Tremendous tolerance for reinvention.

**#I grew a "fuck you" attitude after certain family members
on my biological father's side stole my inheritance.**

#I'm so dumb and naïve sometimes, it's embarrassing.

**#I'm surprised (but not shocked) I figured out
how to build a business without a college degree.**

**#I believe that the world is in deep shit,
and we should lead with kindness
and all put our guns down.**

#I should have been less moody to my parents growing up.

**#I am a dreamer who doesn't believe
that dreams can't come true.**

#I don't want to die alone.

The intention of this exercise is to convince you that creating a personal hashtag list takes your sh*t to a different, concrete level. Once you write the one-liners reflecting the good and the bad about yourself, and really get a read on who you are, and if you're a decent person who cares (at least a little), I'm sure you'll work hard to turn the negative around, or at least own your crap.

#I don't want to be known as a crazy person. Just eccentric!

#What's your sh*t?

Do you have the gumption to hear from a friend that you're a manipulator? Can you handle your parents telling you to your face that you're a pain? Do you have the courage to admit you're too lazy to fulfill your true potential? Why don't you finally admit that your kids are losers? It's not your fault they're deadbeats, but they are—and they need to leave your house because you are crippling them, and the little angels are killing you too.

#It ain't mean to come clean...with yourself.

Speaking of coming clean, here's a wacky exercise I go through, using only a pad and pen—or a tablet or smartphone if my carpal tunnel syndrome isn't acting up. (Joke.)

When the chips are down and you need a boost, write down the following phrases. Fill up the page as much as possible—I know you'll be amazed how good you feel after thoughtfully adding up all the good that comes from you:

Here's the first phrase:

"I am talented and unique because I [and then *you* fill in the blank.]

Here are some other examples:

"I am talented and unique because I [was top in my Latin class.]"

"I am thoughtful and caring because [I fixed the neighbor's broken window and didn't want their kids to get cut on the glass.]"

"I am loving and kind because I [found my significant other's birthstone and had the jeweler make a heart out of it for her milestone birthday.]"

If you think putting a list together like this is corny, then I demand you to go back and read "Step One: Dream Big!," because it seems as if you can't get out of your own jaded way and try something new. Puhleese already. Stop it!!

What's healing about this exercise is that when you write things down, it turns into a contract between you and you. It's a purely personal proclamation: no one but you has to know about your innermost thoughts; you don't have to share this with anyone else. Once you realize the page is packed with great kudos attached to your name, I promise you will get out of your own way—shake off your funk and start to smile.

On the flip side of the coin, not everyone is sweet, smart and caring—at least, not all the time. (I know I'm not.)

Get out your pad again. This time, use a separate page from the accolades. Here are some examples where your description about yourself might not be flattering; however, once you admit your mistakes, you will be on the road to healing.

Here goes:

"I'm not that nice when [I tattled on my friend to our Spanish teacher.]

I was really self-centered when [I walked out of my parents' anniversary party when they asked me to turn off my cellphone.]

And if you're really digging this exercise, and you know you can be bitter, vicious and hateful, go bold and keep scribbling:

"I am a real jerk because I [didn't tell my friend I found the hundred bucks he lost at his birthday party.]"

I am careless when I [was texting while driving.]

I was a snob when I [told my best friend her wedding gown looked cheap—just minutes before she was about to walk down the aisle.]

Again, writing something about yourself, where you can see it as a proclamation, helps you to focus on what it is you like or dislike about yourself more clearly.

#If you took the time to *write*, you're on the road to *right*.

The upside of knowing your sh*t is that you have the power and ability to change (if you want or need to), put out the gossip fire, stopping your "frenemies" from talking about you behind your back—and, most importantly, avoiding any painful surprises. If someone is talking behind your back, blow their cover and say, "Hey, I know I can be a bit of an asshole, but let's take your and my name out of this...and when you get a chance, please let me know if you think it's appropriate in business to walk out of your job without meeting a deadline or giving your supervisor the courtesy of letting them know so that they could get someone else to help." At the end of a conversation when you clearly humble yourself and let the world know your sh*t, your adversary will say, "Wow, even though I really do think he's arrogant, he was spot on."

#Be two steps ahead of your emotions and your critics, not two steps in the dark.

Here's another freeing exercise—especially if you're a carefree and clueless person who wonders why you don't have many friends (and want them). I know you've got at least one confidant, right? (If not, I'll sign up!) Seriously, ask them what they think people like or dislike about you. And you know what I always say, you don't have to worry about The Friggen' Joneses, but it's always interesting to hear what a good, trusted person will reveal. They'll help you discover things you might not know about yourself. Ask them to help you decipher your strengths and weaknesses. You'd be surprised what you might hear, like:

Did you know you get sloppy when you drink?

When you smile, you light up the room.

You are so super-skinny. You're starting to look unhealthy.

Have you noticed you're still limping after football practice? Is it time to go to the doctor?

Even though you're the smartest in the class, your attitude sucks.

You have a flair for taking the simplest clothes and making them look expensive.

I really think you should be nicer to your mother. She was only trying to help you—not hurt you.

You always complain about your age, but you look amazing! Everyone at the club is so jealous.

Have you seen the way he/she looks at you?

Did you know you're an absolute knockout?

And the list, I'm sure, can go on!

Knowing your sh*t is the ticket to deleting the statements you don't like about yourself and beefing up the ones you're in love with. If you don't want people to think you're a procrastinator, get your ass up and arrive on time. If you don't want to be known as a schmuck, go cold turkey and turn into an angel. You'll be surprised how much support you'll find out there, if you just come clean and be honest and transparent with yourself and others.

An honest self-checkup is a major step forward towards getting out of your own way. If you really want to get over your never-ending bullshit, it's time to **"TAKE-A-QUIZ"** and meet your demons:

1. **Do you have the capability to expose your strengths and weaknesses?** Take your emotional inventory seriously and have the gumption to look yourself in the eye and let yourself and others know what you like or don't like about yourself. Remember that many, if not all people have skeletons in our closets that keep us human. If you don't like something you do, chances are others don't either. So stop picking your nose or biting your nails or gossiping—for Pete's sake, get rid of those bad habits already. Make the lists I spoke about. They work.

2. **Can you finally flush your pebbles of emotional sh*t down the toilet?** Puhleese, cross the bad, stupid, unnecessary nitpicking about your poor, sad self off the list immediately! We're all so tired of hearing you still owe student loans or hate your job. Put your grown-up pants on and shut the fuck up about your problems. Get epic: find bigger ideas and broader descriptions about who you really are. People will be more interested in you,

because you'll exude an interest, a mystique—not turn people off.

3. **Are you smart enough to be two steps ahead of your frenemies?** Put out the fire of gossip by telling everyone that "Yes, I was chosen out of a thousand people and got the job" or "Yes, I did a sex tape when I was twenty-one—that was thirty years ago—no need to whisper. Do you want a copy?" Honestly, that'll shut up your so-called "friends." They'll finally leave you alone because, frankly, if you beat them at their petty game, they will have nothing else to say about you.

4. **Do you have the capacity to change your life up based on where you are on the journey?** If Demi can go from superstar to super government employee—and put money down on a townhouse to boot—you can too. We all have different needs at different times of our lives. Once you become your biggest fan, you'll know what you need, and when.

5. **How do you handle anger?** Brewing in anger is a cancer diagnosis waiting to happen. Let off some steam, put your emotional guns down, and release all that inner drama that stops you dead in your tracks, unable to bypass your demons. Punch a pillow. You'll be amazed how much lighter you will feel.

We all come with the bizarre and the amazing. The more you know about yourself, the more you have the power to move all the negative traits off the first Google page about you. Optimize your own search engine and fill up your emotional website with great posts. As soon as you come to terms with who you really are, you'll be on the path you're meant to live by. It might sound old-school, but it takes as much energy to fuck yourself up as it does to do the right thing—all for the sake of growing up and being a kind, responsible adult.

Step Five:

Own the Power of Thoughtfulness

If you're thinking that this is where I'm going to get all woo-wooish, with snippets of sunrises and pansies, think again. That does *not* mean I don't like a good Pilates class, a hot cup of green tea, a cold glass of green juice, a relaxing meditation, or a walk on the beach to reflect. In this Step, we're simply going to take a journey up and down the streets of everywhere in order to navigate those entities who are or aren't thoughtful. After reading some of these snippets, you'll find your own power of thoughtfulness to help you:

#Be a better person.

**#Think calmly and thoughtfully
as you make your next move in life.
(Or change up the one you're in now.)**

It's amazing how thoughtfulness is weaved in and out of our day, and our lives. Most of us might not realize it, but the act of being thoughtful or careless can make or break major world and personal events.

Here is an example of kind gestures that work wonders with people:

#"Hello!"

#"Please"

#"Thank you"

#"My pleasure"

#"Whatever you need, I'm here!"

It is sad to think that we're in a state where we have to remind people of those gestures, but no judgment. Better late than never to give good thoughtfulness responses a try.

On the other side of the spectrum, here is an example of communication that really doesn't encourage anyone to listen further to you:

#"Get your ass up and get me a beer."

#"Shut the fuck up. You're a piece of shit for lying to me."

#"You don't know what the hell you're talking about."

#"Are you crazy?"

#"No one cares what you think because you're nothing to this family."

Becca (aka "Becky") was a kind-hearted woman in her thirties; however, she gave away too much of her downtime to her abusive seventy-eight-year-old mother and dismissive eighty-year-old father—both of whom treated her like dirt. Neighbors used to call her "Beccarella" because she was her family's version of Cinderella, no doubt. Even though Becky worked out her deep-seated issues with her therapist, it was still hard for her to constantly hear her mother call her "useless" and "a piece of shit," when Becky was the sole breadwinner for the family! (That mother was a bitchy brainwasher, for sure.)

Becky could afford to live on her own, but her constant "what-if" guilt stopped her from moving out and developing healthy relationships with people. ("What if I left and my mother died on the floor?" "What if I moved out and my father was found missing in an alcoholic stupor?")

Although Becky thought her patience for putting up with her despicable parents was thoughtful, it was actually very thoughtless—because it put her health and well-being second to the welfare of people who blatantly thought she was worthless.

#Imagine how thoughtless acts
disguise themselves as thoughtful.

#Treat others as you would like to be treated.

In my opinion, the downfall of the many moving parts of thoughtfulness, surprisingly, comes from television. The cable and news networks are sooo niched out, we're all gravitating to news we want to hear, not news we have to think about and maybe disagree with. Have you ever flipped channels between CNN and FOX News Channel? Both networks report on virtually the same story (when the government allows CNN in to hear the press conference), but each one has its particular

spin, which too often leaves the viewer without a full report.
I remember following the first hundred days of President
Trump's term on TV and flipping between channels—one
showed protests and the other showed the President signing
bills in an office. Really, networks? Imagine a world where CNN
and FOX News merged. Would they be called "Fort NNox?"
I'd love a split screen to hear and watch the same story told by
these two networks—can you imagine all the spin that will be
splattered on the screen?

Does the media think Americans have so little capacity for
thought that they can't hear *all* the sides of the story? (Long
ago, back in the days of Walter Cronkite, reporters took pride in
balanced reporting. Really.) Now, it seems as if we all are either
news junkies or can't stand to hear anything about the news.
With all the news and the hype and the breaking news, which,
many times, isn't that breaking at all, it's mind-boggling to
think that people are being lured to a network by the look and
the personal life of a news reader. Are we that shallow? Why
should we trust someone because of their sexual orientation,
or want to hear the news from someone who lied about a
past story they wrote? Why should we listen to someone who
exudes his personal opinion in the story? The American media
has turned news into entertainment, with a diverse cast of
characters as if we're watching a movie. (I love watching that
guy with the lisp! What's her hair going to look like in this
show? She has such white teeth. I love it when she snickers
and laughs—she should be doing sitcoms, not the six o'clock
report.) Media has an ethical responsibility to present the news
on an even playing field so that viewers can thoughtfully weigh

the pros and cons and reach their own conclusion. Imagine if the news were given like it was an audition for a classical orchestra where the news reader reports behind a black curtain, and all the viewer had to do was *listen?* (Did you know some orchestras hold "blind" auditions where musicians play behind a curtain so that the sound, not gender or other bias, is the deciding factor to who's accepted or not?)

**#I trust her news reports because
I like the way she sits on the chair and crosses her legs.**

**#He tells me the truth because
he wears an American Flag on his lapel.**

**#He didn't know how to fact check because
he didn't know what a real fact was.**

Wouldn't it be refreshing if we all were able to talk politics without raising our blood pressure? Wouldn't it be more thoughtful if our politicians remembered they are *civil servants* and not above us all—doing us a favor for taking a press conference? Wouldn't it be dandy if we could have a thoughtful discussion about current events without the fear of friends and family members shunning us because we don't think like them?

# # #

The following subjects I bring up are just a launchpad for other scenarios where thoughtfulness should take place. Hopefully, these what-could-seem really trite hashtags can expand your idea that small, thoughtful gestures go a big way with people who need help:

**#He made sure the batteries fit the flashlight
before selling them to the elderly woman.**

**#She parked close to the front door
so that Granny could get out closer to the restaurant.**

**#I changed the plans from vacation to staycation
because not everyone could afford to travel.**

**#He reminded his aunt to bring all her medications
so that the doctor wouldn't overprescribe.**

**#She remembered her sister loved tiger lilies
and sent them to her for her birthday.**

**#He made sure they went to a romantic movie
and not a doomsday massacre for their anniversary.**

#He cooked breakfast for his dad on Father's Day.

**#He held her peacefully
after she received a brain tumor diagnosis.**

#Thoughtfulness is infectious.

I'm sure that we everyday folks have a ton of thoughtful gestures to put on our mantles. Let's look at Carlos, who got a bad deal when his parents divorced. His dad never spoke to him after the dad bimbo'ed with another woman and left to start a new family, and his mom was too busy to help him out because she was working two jobs to support him and his sister, Karlita.

Instead of wearing the "woe-is-me" badge, parading around with a chip on his shoulder, Carlos decided to turn his own scenario around to work in his and his family's favor. Number One: he got a job after school, three times a week, to help his mom pay the phone and heating bills. He knew he couldn't pay more, but he figured if he could help the family out strategically, it would be less of a burden on his mother. Number Two: he helped his mom and sister cook on Sundays, in order to have food ready for the week. He was tired of eating those overly processed fast foods, and by helping his family make meals, everyone had more leisure time, and got a wholesome, hot meal every night. Another win/win.

Carlos helped Karlita with her homework, because her grades were falling off—was it because their father ditched them? Carlos wasn't made of steel, but he was smart enough to realize that he and Karlita were not responsible for their dad's cheating escapades and could do something to get his sister back on track.

Every night, Carlos made a point to wish his mother and sister good night, and tell them both he loved them.

#Great families can come in small packages

#Thoughtfulness is a sign of love.

Let's talk about how thoughtlessness has become part of
how companies deal with their customers. When I sit on the
phone with three or four customer service reps from around
the globe, each one less capable and more inaudible than the
last, I look up to the sky four hours later and wonder: How
has the planet gotten so off mark when it comes to the most
important part of a service industry, marketing and customer
support? All these reps seem to be scripted by the same person
who rehearsed Susan Bennett, the original voice of Siri. Susan
seems like a nice, practical lady; however, when it comes to
those who work at Apple, as cute as their products are, a lot of
their functionality and marketing techniques seem impractical.
First, I find it outrageous that Apple tests their equipment
on the consumer *after* we buy it. In my opinion, it's as if a
frenemy invites you over for brunch and feeds you raw eggs in
an omelet. Second, when Apple releases a new product, why
do they ditch a lot of their much-needed accessories that they
made you purchase for the last model, forcing you to have to
buy new plugs and prongs—thus racking up more money on the
already-supercharged invoice? Is all the changeup in the spirit
of new technology? Spare me the technobabble as I hand over
my credit card.

Have you ever been on the phone with Apple technical support?
In my experience, Apple has a three-step customer support
process before you can get a serious problem solved. I'm not
talking about adding an email address on an iPad. I'm talking
about when you must configure a new device that you spent

hundreds and hundreds of dollars on only to know you're going to have to spend hours, sometimes days on figuring out how to set it up so you can use it. I am so worn out from all the Apple configuration gymnastics, I seriously think twice about buying a new product because the set-up is so painful. Did you read that, Apple?

#Configuration is a bitch.

In the world of Apple support, first you're introduced to a screener—most likely a kid whose parents were hippies; you can tell just by the way they speak. Then you're sent to a junior rep who only seems to know five steps of how to solve a problem. And then, you're put on hold for a senior rep—only to be cut off because of a poor cell connection! (Ugh, that has happened to me more than I'd care to believe. Should I move to a place where they have better cell service simply to support Apple customer support?) You'd think that the rep, who knows everything about you, including your name, your sex, your address, and your phone number, would call you back—but most of the time, they don't. So, you must climb up the heap of help again and kind of start all over. It's so annoying when an automated attendant asks you for the serial number, and the real live screener asks you for the same thing! If all of these companies value automated attendants, why don't they trust their robot has taken the correct information for you? They could use technology to help improve the experience. And then, hours later, once the senior advisor fixes the problem but tells you he/she needs to "do more research" on the secondary issue at hand, and plans a follow-up call, you're forced to climb up the Matterhorn again because the advisor almost never can speak on the day and time they've booked with you. Good luck with missing their call. Even if you call back the second they hang up, and say, "Hey I was just in the bathroom when you called—here I am...can you talk?" Not. Now that's customer service!

How about those lovely people at Spectrum, formerly known as Time Warner (Huge Entitlement) Cable? Those *yahoos* (and I'm not talkin' about the Internet portal) never cease to amaze me. One day they're the "Only Game in Town" cable company and the next they're "No Obligation" cable. How do they have the nerve to raise a rate by two hundred dollars for the same services, simply because a contract is up? I always feel as if I'm a skydiver in freefall mode when I try and renegotiate with them after a contract is up. Now that they are promoting no-contract services, it's "one for all and all for one". When you make the case against the outrageous bill they sent you, they admit to lowering the fees but further turn the screw by telling you that "now we have established your new price: please wait for an email from our billing department, which totals up your revised bill with the tax." When you ask them, "What happens until then?" the nerves inside you throb even more as they answer, "The (inflated) price remains the same until you get a confirmation that the new 'lower' price has been processed." When you have the strength to close your mouth in disgust and ask them if they could simply tally up the fees and the state tax (and give you the price over the phone), they act like little termites eating through your wooden support beams and say,

"I wish I had a tax calculator here...you don't know how many people ask the same question."

Does Time Warner Cable...uh, *Spectrum*...really think their marketing tactics put the customer first? Perhaps they're so burned out because with all the other services like Amazon and Netflix, they know it's only a matter of time before their jig is up.

When it comes to customer support, I truly believe that Spectrum is one of the most thoughtless companies in this country.

#Speak to the customer
as if you're speaking to your best friend.

Another confusing company to work with is Network Solutions—they provide email hosting among other things. If your email system goes down, you call a rep. At first, they seem nice enough on the phone and understand your complaint, but wait.... Then *they*, not you, start typing the issue to their IT support department, and then you're in the hands of someone to whom you've never spoken to—and many times you're forced to hang up the phone without any resolution, for the most part, and pray that someone behind a virtual velvet rope will solve the issue and come to the rescue. Why on Earth would NetSol hire customer support reps to type to other customer support staff your issue at hand? Weird.

My young reader friends here are probably saying, "What is he going on and on about?" Young people can't understand the power of thoughtfulness when it comes to customer service, because they've never lived in a world where companies took pride in their products. In fact, in the world of electronics they have forced customers to "type" their customer-related issues rather than spend less than forty-five seconds allowing them to chat with real people—real adults who have better things to do than hang out on a phone and listen to pop, jazz, or classical music while waiting. Honestly, those big businesses that supported Donald Trump's "Make America Great Again" campaign should employ more reps in the *United States* and:

#Make customer support great again.

I think the most frustrating customer service calls I ever had were with Sleep Number—the bed people. For a little less than 5K (and in my humble opinion as a consumer), two blow-up rafts and some foam rubber arrived in my apartment with a mechanism that masqueraded as a bed frame. When I saw these two dudes inflating these sleep chambers, I thought I was going to have a convulsion and throw myself on the street waiting for the trucks to drive over me because the price and product didn't seem to add up. After these rafts were nipped and tucked into their foam cover, I was given a lesson in how to use the remote—I'm sure you've heard that you can customize the firmness of each side of the bed. That means that there's an air pump which can inflate or deflate the rafts based on your preferred sleep number. Once the installers left, the problems began immediately: my remote got stuck, and they didn't tell me that if you have duo chambers and you don't have a partner in bed with you (on the other side, thank you very much), the bed becomes lopsided if you don't position both chambers on the same sleep setting. Imagine being a "10," and trying to turn your body and move to the other side of the bed when it's a "45?" During my time with Sleep Number, I had been on the phone with them for probably 420 minutes—seven phone calls, each of which took about an hour. Finally, when I was ready to return this floating device (again, this is from my vantage point), they said, "We can return the mattresses, but we can't return the bedframe because it's considered 'furniture,' and when you signed your contract, it says that 'furniture' can't be returned."

For once, I had the upper hand against a company that was one step from—I thought—scamming me because of their small print. I was so crazed that these people had the nerve to tell me they can't return part of their device, I sought out the CEO on LinkedIn, asking for her help; suddenly, I received a call from a "senior" rep who was more than happy to troubleshoot. She too, in a gentler tone, told me that the bedframe was nonreturnable; however, what the rep(s) didn't realize (which would be disturbing to me if I was the CEO) was that I *never* signed a contract. So, this company *had to* return everything back with a full refund—something that they should have done within their grace period anyway, no questions asked.

#Companies should never put a consumer through unnecessary drama.

#The customer is always right.

It's mind-boggling to think that those in power—from news organizations to tech companies, from box stores to politicians, and from everyday people to strangers—find the power of thoughtfulness over greed challenging. Everyone should find the "Carlos" inside of them and extend goodwill. I really believe that regardless of what side of the fence we are on—the political aisle or a customer service call—we all want to get out of our way so we can be better people. Is that a pipe dream, or can I hear a hell-yeah?! Here's a **"TAKE-A-QUIZ"** I hope will be helpful for you:

1. **Do you really need a script to be kind to one another?** Look at the issue at hand as if you're helping your best friend or a family member. Deal with life's challenges that are happening here and now, and get off the wrong message points!

2. **How many times during the day do you do a good deed or put your best foot forward for others?** The power of extending thoughtfulness to others is angelic—truly good for the soul, and good for the body too. After doing something nice for someone else will you feel great, and whomever you've helped will also get a feel-great jolt.

3. **Do you have the courage to turn on media outlets you supposedly don't agree with to see another perspective?** Expand your news sources so that you can hear *all* points of view before you come to your own thoughtful conclusion. You're smarter than you think, and as long as we're still considered a free society, revel in the blanket of diversity and see life from all different angles.

4. **Are you defensive when confrontation heats up?**
   Cool down and remember to use thoughtful words when
   you're in a disagreement. After all, your "opponent" isn't
   out to kill you. (If they are, run and call 911!) Seriously
   though, words and phrases like, "Respectfully," "I
   really need your help in understanding," "I know you
   feel differently about the way this turned out...," or
   even acknowledging the person by saying, "Thank you
   for taking the time to think about this," and even the
   best, most humble phrase, like "I apologize," will go a
   long way and get both of you to think thoughtfully—
   and harmoniously.

5. **Are you comfortable giving compliments?** Make
   a point to give a nice compliment to someone when its
   due...it will help open them up to seeing you as a nice
   person. Remember: there's a time and a place to tell a
   woman that she has beautiful legs or a guy that he has big
   guns. (I'm sure you know that it's NOT in the workplace!)

I can't say enough about how the power of thoughtfulness is the
key to living with others and taking pride in everything you do.
If you make a habit of thinking twice about littering or reacting
to someone else's road rage, no one will have to tell you what's
the right or wrong way, because you'll be ahead of the curve.
And if being thoughtful seems corny to others—too goody-two-
shoes for them—well, that's their problem.

Waking up in a thoughtful state of mind puts us on a high
road and sends a message to others to meet us on the same
wavelength. It's easy to blow a gasket, and Lord only knows,

we are all guilty of giving in to selfish impulses and negative emotions. If we can all give ourselves the courtesy to think before we speak, the world would be in a better place, our relationships would flourish, and we would extend goodwill to others that will leave us feeling content and "heard."

Step Six:

Learn How to Communicate

Communication nowadays is so "white noisy," don't you think? There are so many ways to do it—it's crazy. After sitting back and watching these communicative gadgets explode right in front of me, I'm not convinced that all of them are necessary. Perhaps you think differently, but I find myself in a pinball maze of chatter with people numerous times of the day— pulling me from one device to another, as if I'm a yo-yo in an "around-the-world" trick. This one texts; that one only emails; the other one calls at all hours of the night, leaves a message, and then emails the rest of the day. I promise you that I'm not irrelevant when I say that my secret wish is that we rewind the tape and get these freaking cellphones, laptops, and apps semi-permanently out of our lives—let's treat them like the liquor blue laws where you can't use them on a Sunday. (*Joke!* Kinda.)

#How *do* you spell "communicate?" C-O-N-F-U-S-I-N-G...

...That's how you spell this debacle we're in. It's mind-boggling that in this day and age—and with all the different ways the electronics industry has sold e-tools with the supposed purpose of making talking with people more convenient—we don't seem to understand each other most of the time. I've heard that one in ten kids are addicted to video games and couldn't care less about being humanly social—gosh, that means a gazillion kids don't go out and play ball, ride bikes, or just plain talk to others? If they're going to be anti-social hermits and lock themselves in their bedrooms all weekend, can't their parents (who have participated in making them little monsters, BTW) at least text little Joey and tell him to open a window, air out his room, and get the dirty laundry off the floor? Sheesh.

The history of communication, in a 140-character-like nutshell, is a bit like building a sandwich. First, the cavemen carved in stone (only the anthropologists and geeks know if they grunted or did other things to get attention); then, our forefathers spoke and wrote letters; then, our grandfathers spoke, called on the phone, wrote letters, and used a typewriter; and, of course, our parents spoke, called on the phone, wrote letters, many used a typewriter, and some used a Wang word processor.

Now, all hell has broken loose.

To communicate, we text, post, Instagram, Snapchat, Periscope (Hmmm. Did that one take off like the company had hoped?), Skype, email, call—maybe write a postcard!

By the time this book is published, perhaps some of those platforms will be obsolete?

Speaking of hell, I had a teeny, tiny, snooty thirtysomething client named "Ramona," a celebrity Pilates instructor, who literally got in her own way when she started believing her own PR. After she was featured in one of the fancy newspapers, you would have thought that Beyoncé was now signed to my roster. (I wish!) While she was acting out her PR fantasies, she decided to scrap what we were hired to do, and ask me if we were interested in planning her engagement party in a month and her "destination" wedding in six months— consisting of adventure and "glamping" activities. (Apparently, she just got engaged the night before and her decision to switch our contract was a "take it or leave it" proposition.) Since I helped to plan a ton of weddings at Triplets and had just helped to coordinate a gay one at my company, this was a no-brainer, even though my gut told me we had a chokingly tight timeline, since most couples book venues a year in advance. Oh, and our mission was to try and get everything deeply discounted, because Ra-Ra felt her number of social media followers (just barely reaching six figures, which in today's virtual world is still a bit novice), warranted cheaper rates. I and my staff love a challenge and are great at getting scrappy when we are handed a nearly unattainable task. With that kind of pressure, we all needed to be in constant contact with Ra-Ra because, some of the venues on her wishlist might have a last minute cancellation—and if so, Ra needed to act fast and put down the deposit to hold the date. (Did I tell you I actually gave a venue our business credit card to hold a spot for Ra?) *One more thing:* Did I also mention she wanted us to book an *entire* weekend of activities *and* to, top it off, it had to be a macrobiotic affair?! In about three days, my staff delivered a list of twenty destination spots. One in particular had the perfect weekend available, but we needed to get a hold of Queen Ra-Ra's royal arse and talk logistics. Where the fuck is "Ra-Ra?" Where the crap is her fiancé, Bam-Bam? (Bam was the guy who chewed us out the night before because he said we didn't *understand* how to pitch Ra to a venue—even though we had worked with this chick for a year already and got her top-notch media coverage.) According to Ra, Bam was her backup if she wasn't available; however, he didn't respond either.

Finally, hours and hours later we hear back from Ra-

Ra who, incidentally, had a huge chip on her shoulder when we finally spoke (the reason she didn't respond) because she felt that speaking on the phone, ("Ra, please call us asap—we found the venue—time sensitive..."), rather than texting, was irrelevant and made us look "antiquated." Ra-Ra told me that if texting was a good enough communications tool for her agents, she didn't need to speak with us on the phone! Really, Ra-Ra? The last time I checked, your agents weren't returning your calls, let alone planning your glamping, macrobiotic wedding weekend, and asking you to plop down thousands of dollars for a deposit. Do you really think that a sane human being can carry out a business discussion about *your* wedding solely over text or email?

It's so funny that B-Listers demand more diva attention than many of the big celebs.

Even though we found a caterer, a free liquor sponsor, a free photographer for the engagement party (all within a week!), *and* even though we found some great venues who agreed to throw a macrobiotic shindig, as well as convinced a celebrity dress designer to barter a free wedding gown for Pilates classes, Ra-Ra fired us because of our *communications skills*—she didn't care if we made tremendous headway in finding the dream venue for her. ("I now pronounce Ra-Ra a [fill in the blank].")

Sadly, "Ra-Ra" Ramona missed out on a tremendous

opportunity that we could have handled for her, if we had been given the courtesy to have ten minutes on the phone with her to decipher what all her three-word texts meant.

#Speaking is not old-school and antiquated.

According to the Pew Research Center's *Internet & American Life Project*, thirty-one percent of those surveyed nationwide said they preferred texting over talking. Pew goes on to say that "cell owners between the ages of eighteen and twenty-four exchange an average of 109.5 messages on a normal day—that works out to more than thirty-two hundred texts per month—and the typical or median cell owner in this age group sends or receives fifty messages per day (or fifteen hundred messages per month)." With all those thumbprint gymnastics, it's no wonder people are tricked into thinking they're actually having conversations. Am I wrong to assume that "Facetime" doesn't substitute for organic, touchy-feely *Realtime?* I'm sure we've all been in circumstances where meeting people in the flesh adds a more dynamic, meaningful introduction than simply meeting on email.

Imagine if someone who made a living in communications for decades—like me—didn't know how to communicate. Ruthless Ramona was so silly even pretending she was "one-upping" her branding firm. The truth was:

#She wasn't interested in *listening, she loved to dictate.*

What Ra-Ra forgot (or perhaps she never learned it from her parents) was that communicating is a two-way process, where the rhythm of the act is as important as the act itself. When you only text, you're forced to stop—then start—then pick up the next day, and in many cases, end a conversation without closure.

#Texting an important conversation stints the two-way act of communicating.

Her attitude towards us was as if we had just killed her unborn child. Her stubbornness got in her own way, and once she started sinking in her own quicksand of inflexibility, she was drowned in frustration. To this day, *no one* is working with Ramona because she has an abominable reputation.

#Don't get in the way of those who want you to be success. They're not your enemy.

As previously mentioned, it's clear we're being sold *products* for the "luxury" of communicating in the modern world, regardless as to whether the communication we're doing isn't effective and leaves us empty. Don't get me wrong. As I hinted in the Intro, I love to shop and I love me some gadgets; however, when the gadgets run you instead of the other way around, you're in a dangerous position—and something's wrong with the picture. Who the hell wants to be told they have only 140 characters to "chat" with people and only twenty-four hours until that cutesy video they made disintegrates? Are we all twelve, needing someone to tell us how to relate to each other? Isn't that rather invasive? What about our privacy? It seems as if all these social media platforms make rules as if they're playing a board game like Monopoly.

**#Celebrate International Privacy Awareness Day
by raising awareness of privacy issues.**

#Communication is the key to getting out of your own way.

#She broke up with her fiancé via text.

#He received his pink slip via email.

We're all sitting on subways, on buses, in elevators, and on planes without any communicative skills towards one another, as if the "Candy Crush" game is more important than human interaction. For those living in a big city, have you noticed that mostly no one reads the traditional news or book formats on public transportation any longer? In the old days (seven years ago, perhaps...is that old?), people would stretch out the Sunday newspaper so they could experience the big, bold, vista of the story, spread out across two pages.

**#Reading a newspaper on the smartphone
is as if you're ogling a stripper through a peep-hole.**

The smartphone isn't the only way to dehumanize people.

Frank was a twentysomething waiter, who was burned out from waiting tables. Waitering was an ultimate challenge for Frank because he was painfully shy and hated dealing with people. As a way of suppressing his anxiety, Frank stayed up all night, playing video games—leaving no energy left for the daytime. At family functions, Frank would go to the corner and play games on his tablet, rarely looking up or speaking. It was as if he was a ghost floating through the hallways, observing but not participating. How could friends and family put up with this horrible, self-destructive behavior? How could they allow an adult to exude such bad social skills? How can Frank get out of his own late-night way? (Aren't twentysomethings considered adults, or did the government raise the age to forty?)

In a therapy session, Frank told the counselor he was comfortable interacting with "friends" during the night as he played games. The therapist asked if he ever met these "friends" of his, and he awkwardly replied, "No, but I know we'd *be* friends if we met in person."

**#Are friends you've never met
outside of the Internet real friends?**

**#Smartphones and laptops are becoming
the next version of crack.**

How super-sad it was for Frank, that he never experienced real interaction with others. And *that* is precisely why anyone who has lived in a land of authenticity needs to help those who can't get out of their own head, which can be a terrible, lonely way of getting in your own way. Stand out for being socially adaptable, not disconnected. If you're super shy and really want to challenge yourself, rehearse "small talk" party conversation in front of a mirror so that you're prepared to speak. We've all heard of those who aspire to be recording artists, and sing in front of the mirror holding a hairbrush for a mic. Now we're at the point where we have to stand in front of the mirror, and prep how to talk to one another! We are really in Loserville.

Frank is far from the only Millennial I've met who suffers from communication challenges. In my business, I actually had to teach a twentysomething staffer how to address an envelope. First, his handwriting was that of a ten-year-old, and second, he had no idea the order in which the contact info appeared. *This is ridiculous.* Whoever is teaching children in schools should be ashamed of themselves. Doesn't the "core curriculum," or whatever the hell it's called, teach cursive handwriting any longer? Sure, it's easy to print out a label, but when this dude gets engaged to be married is his fiancée going to address stickers slapped on the custom-engraved Papyrus invitations—or will she want beautiful calligraphy? Incidentally, when you're lucky enough to go to a function like a wedding, a graduation, etc., when you leave the party, pop a handwritten card in the mail and thank the host for having you. Your "thank you" card will forever etch yourself in the "good guest" category.

#If you can't rely on what God gave you first, you're fucked when there's a power outage.

#At thirty-five, he questioned why she needed a real birthday card, even though his e-card went into spam.

I can't believe that writing a handwritten note is on the brink of extinction. Have you ever smiled when you got a real, touchy-feely, wacky birthday card that popped up when you opened the envelope, or stopped in your tracks when a heartfelt condolence card came on special, exotic grass paper adorned with gold leaf? Writing a letter or a card to someone represents an amount of time someone devoted *just for you*—first, it takes time to find the most appropriate card, then it takes time to inscribe it, not to mention mailing it. It's like a long-lost ritual. Sadly, we have depleted ourselves of the nuances of communication by condensing and acronym-izing what was once a rich and robust exchange between each other. We pretty much don't take ownership of the written word. We've settled for hiding behind or dumbing down our thoughts—all for the convenience of using electronic devices that we think will do most of the job for us.

I feel truly blessed to have lived a life filled with genuine, face-to-face social exchanges, like this one, dedicated to anyone who has ever loved a dog:

One day, my little Scottie dog, Lester, threw up a quarter-sized amount of blood. I took him to the hospital where the vet said that he probably had an upset stomach. Later that night, Lester was getting worse. I brought him to an emergency room, because Lester was definitely not himself. He was making sounds that I never heard, as if he was saying, "Daddy, I'm scared. Help me. Help me." Once Lester was admitted to the hospital, all was calm, collected. The doctor suggested I stick around in the waiting room just to see how things were going to progress.

This was all scary to me. I was used to being cautious when it came to health issues, almost in a frozen state. However, the sounds Lester made—face-to-face—prompted me to step out of my own slow-mo mode and get him help.

Fifteen minutes before the hospital was closing for the night, the vet tech called me back to see Lester, who at that point, went from a feisty, friendly little Scottie to an ill dog, with monitors and feeding tubes poked into every crevice of his body. "How did he get like this?" I thought.

When Lester saw me, he picked himself up, tried to pull off all the catheters, and came over to me with a look I'd never seen before.

I could have sworn a tear dropped out of the corner of his eye.

Though his eyes didn't look their normal deep bold, blue/brown/black any longer, there was a sparkle —almost like a halo shooting out of his retina. The most amazing thing about animals is that they speak with their eyes, and at that moment, Lester was talking to me: as if asking for my permission to pass away. I looked at him squarely, and whispered in his ear, "It's OK, Lester. Let go. I love you and I will see you soon, somewhere, somehow. It's OK."

Lester took whatever he thought I said as an invitation to move out of his body and into another one; however, at that moment, it wasn't as maudlin as one would think. He didn't die. He took a deep breath, as if he was my grandfather ready to say a prayer before a family dinner, and went from limp to Lester again! He went to the corner of his huge patient cage and sat, trying to pull out the feeding tubes, and blinking his eyes as if he was a puppy who saw the light for the first time.

The vet said, "Well, he's looking much better to me. It's time for us to close, but I'll make sure you get access to see him first thing in the morning."

As soon as I returned home—about twenty-five minutes or so after seeing my little Lester come "back" from death, I got the call that Lester died. He gave me the gift of his life for five amazing years, and heard every word I said till the end.

Imagine having a conversation with Lester like this on Skype? I don't think so. Frankly, that conversation with Lester was more thoughtful than the ones we tried to have with Ra-Ra Ramona. Think about that one.

No discussion about communication would be complete without mentioning the latest bid for the 45th Presidency. (Sorry, people. But I'm bringing up this shit show, with heart and soul, to make a point.) Politics has made the art of communication worthless because what people say and what the transcript states are forever out of balance. Everyone lies, to put it bluntly. In this outrageous presidential race, everyone working for either candidate threw out every ethic their parents taught them (or did their parents teach them anything?) in favor of saying whatever it took to persuade the trusted voters of America to believe them.

#What if the Declaration of Independence
were created on Snapchat and disappeared in a day?

The cast of characters in an election includes candidates, media, their talking heads and opponents, politicians, bloggers, and citizens. Here's what that election between Clinton and Trump will be known for:

#She rarely connected spontaneously with her audience.

#He played dirty to win.

**#They were so desperate for followers
they rarely fact-checked before posting a story.**

#She sounds scripted and robotic.

#He creates controversy to get people to pay attention.

Politicians are, in many ways, the most confusing, and in some cases, the worst communicators on the face of the planet. Everyone involved in this campaign, on both sides, should take the responsibility of admitting how they communicated poorly.

My company once represented a fun party game called "Drunk, Stoned or Stupid," which was anything but. We learned later than sooner that because of some ethics code, the media refused to promote anything with the words "drunk" or "stoned" attached. Are they dirty and offensive words? *Really?*

That same media who pooh-poohed the game was clamoring to air political videos, posts, and transcripts that were so disgusting for any time slot on television, negating the fact that even their own kids were watching.

Here are some real-life quotes from President Trump that aired on primetime television:

"I did try and fuck her. She was married."

"I moved on her like a bitch."

"Grab them by the pussy."

WTF?! That's right—you can't look me in the eye and *forget* that every "dirty" word in those quotes above aired on major networks, as well as appeared in print. Where was the Parents Television Council when children across America were exposed to hearing those clips, over and over again? I would ask any council involved with television ethics to sue whomever allowed that filth to be spewed over the boob tube. I heard a lot of talking heads on TV dismiss the banter as "locker room conversation." I don't think that a show on CNN, FOX, MSNBC, etc., should be compared as if it's a show that aired live from the YMCA, do you?

**#When you hear the same disrespectful F-Bombs
repeated over and over again,
you become numb to its true meaning.**

Just to be clear: I'm no prude and I have heard, and said, probably every disgusting word out there (and then some); however, we have lost the parameters of ethics in this country, and that—in my humble opinion—sets us up for long-term disaster. Is it because someone said these words? *No.* However, it's because we have broken every parental rule handed down to us that says, "There's a time and place for everything." We must thank the media, who, by playing this infamous foul-mouthed transcript, moved the honesty meter for their best interests and not yours (and certainly not for your children).

It was played at the time, and in the matter in which it was presented to the audience, strictly for dirty politics and ratings.

When I heard and saw the transcript with the word "pussy" splattered across my surround sound TV, I remember thinking: we have just shoveled ourselves so deep in a ditch of mediocrity; I have just witnessed a huge shift that seemed worse than the environmental challenges we face.

#Donald Trump would say and do anything to be famous.

# # #

Speaking as not only someone in the communications business but also a citizen, I want every woman and every man who respects women to stop allowing this bad behavior from anyone—the President, the media, your neighbor, your children. I don't care if Trump is President. He has a wife, two ex-wives, and two daughters (one of whom works right beside him in the White House), and he has no right to persuade anyone on the face of the planet that how he speaks about and deals with women, as we have seen numerous times, is in any way allowable. This is *not* about his political platform—and don't you as a reader start in with me with an excuse that I must've voted for "that 'bitch' (as many called Clinton), who had a private email server."

Since this is not a political book, my hope is that those who voted for President Trump don't feel I'm attacking him—even though I am not a fan of his communication skills whatsoever. I am also not a fan of anyone who doesn't fact check. Does everyone know who Sean Spicer is? According to Wikipedia, he is the 30th White House Press Secretary. Gotta love a Long Island boy who graduated with an MA from the Naval War College, stands in front of America, and continues to flummox fact after fact. Remember his account of the Holocaust? If he were the Communications Director of the Naval War College, he would have been fired immediately for his disrespectful missteps. As a matter of fact, if he were a contestant on *The Apprentice*, he would have been "F-I-R-E-D" for not properly preparing for the challenge! Again, *forget* about party affiliation, people! If you or I came to a meeting ill-prepared, we would be out. WTF?!

#We've all heard of Fake News, what about Fake Communication?

#Make America Respect Again.

Now that I've irked the Republicans, let's push a sensitive button with the Dems. News Alert (*yawn*):

#Hillary Clinton is in desperate need of media training.

The woman has had numerous challenges connecting to the audience without sounding as if she was scripted. Why didn't any of her posse give her the 411—and then a 911 reality check that she better let down her hair and get real? Reality TV stars do a better job speaking in front of the camera than Mrs. Clinton—don't you think that would be a big problem when you have tried twice to run for President? Not connecting with her audience gave the impression she didn't care about Americans. And for God's sake: If you lose an election and your fans are waiting for you at an Expo Center, put your big girl cheerleader panties on and show up, be gracious, and thank them for supporting you. Girl, if you ever need a publicist, please call me. Let's get scrappy!

What about the rest of us?

You are lying to me if you don't think it's weird to break up with a serious relationship via text.

Between the phone, email, and texting, Ernest and his realtor, Leslie, really screwed up Ernest's offer when he was buying his latest apartment in Manhattan. Ernest called Leslie and wanted to bid on his dream crash pad. Leslie responded in a text, "What price?" Ernest emailed the terms. Leslie responded by phone. The transaction was stretched over three platforms. Unfortunately, Ernest forgot to check out Leslie's last text before putting in his final bid via email. In the text, Leslie suggested that Ernest split the difference between his and the seller's last offer; however, because Ernest didn't see that text, he told Leslie to respond back to the seller's broker agreeing to pay the *seller's* final price! What a three-ring circus of communication! Even Mr. Trump (putting his real estate hat on) would be appalled.

If you're solely going to communicate using electronics, what will happen if your phone crashes and your emails and texts get wiped out? How will you live?

Trust me, you will live, and it's time to believe it. It's time to start mixing a little bit of old-school communication in with the new. Promise me that you'll make it a point to talk face-to-face with someone candidly—and for *your* sake, put the smartphone away. Become a champion for making way for real time with people, not "let's pretend" time. Are you ready to **"TAKE-A-QUIZ"** on this subject?:

1. **Do you have the courage to talk to people directly, even when in conflict?** Now that we can all hide behind our electronics, have the guts to come out from the virtual dark and deal with a situation with grace and humility. *Never* break up with someone via text. It's tacky.

2. **How many hours a day do you look up and out, and see the world as if it's a jewel in front of you?** Once you close the laptop and look up and out, you'll be amazed how interesting the real world is to you. Take note: the virtual world is *not* the real world.

3. **Do you turn off the phone when you're talking face to face with someone?** Do you really need to take your cell out on a date or invite it to Sunday dinner with your parents? Unless you're a doctor hired to save lives, turn the fucking phone off and give the people whom you love the courtesy of your time.

4. **When was the last time you sent a real "thank-you" note?** You'll be amazed at how people will be impressed by your action, in any social situation. When it comes to business, a simple, handwritten thank you note will speak volumes; you will be set apart from your competition.

5. **Do you use outrageous words, or post absolutely disgusting videos to get attention?** We've all gotten to the point where we're so numb to bad social behavior, nothing shocks us. Give yourself a challenge and disconnect from all forms of media for six months. Turn it all back on and I promise you, you'll be shocked at all the shocking things out there for you, your friends, and your family to witness.

If you zipped through this chapter, please reread. You know, as I do, that all these electronics are hijacking our lives; however, you're not helpless. *Turn them off!* Try your best not to lie to yourself or others, simply because telling a better fake story will automatically buy you a ticket to more followers on social media. The texting thing is going to be outdated soon, so why constantly rely on it? I dare you to start your own campaign to communicate face-to-face, even with your pets and your politicians too—with a huge heart and a dose of soul, and with a healthy opinion.

Step Seven:

Reboot

Reboot is a trendy word for unplugging. I can't believe I'm at the point in my life that I do meditation breathing exercises in the men's room (when no one is looking, of course). To me, time is time, no matter where you are. If I have a chokingly busy day, I will grab a moment and close my eyes.

In 1976 I experienced my first taste of rebooting at Columbia High School, in Maplewood, New Jersey, which I attended from tenth through twelfth grade. I was in the first public high school class in America to study Transcendental Meditation. You read that correctly. While others were taking shop, cooking, mechanics, and football, I was breathing heavily with my eyes closed in class, learning the technique of TM, reading from a very colorful handbook about the benefits of transcending into a very calm space. After school, I would throw a blanket over my head and take in ten to twenty minutes of dark and calmness before doing homework. What would you expect from a school that was the first in the country to close for Earth Day, was the birthplace of Ultimate Frisbee, and taught a lot of peeps who went onto Hollywood? (If you're interested in all of that, I'm sure you can Google it.) All true. Even now when I'm commuting on a train, I can close my eyes listening to one single over and over again, like "I Want You" by Marvin Gaye, and go into a deep cryonic-like suspension, thanks to learning the unplugging technique at an early age.

**#If you don't have time to meditate,
slip into a bathroom stall and catch some ZZZZs.**

Even though I loved to disconnect from it all, life wasn't so perfect during meditation class. I *loved* the teacher's really curly blond hair and deep blue eyes, but I couldn't stand her voice; it was so breathy and secretive-sounding—honestly, the way she taught the class creeped me out: was I taking a relaxation course, or being lured into a cult? After reading and studying that uber-colored, oversized paperback tome of a textbook from beginning to end, the class was told to show up at such-and-such place on a Saturday to be given a unique mantra. It was almost like an initiation, which, from my understanding, sealed the deal between us and the Maharishi Mahesh Yogi, the founder of the movement. What's a mantra? According to Google, it's a word or sound repeated to aid concentration in meditation.

I show up at this location that felt like a funeral home. The whole class gathered in the living room. When the teacher opened the French doors and walked in with a long white robe as if she was auditioning for a gospel choir in Newark, New Jersey, I believed my fears were about to come true: "I'm going to be abducted by a thin white woman who wore no makeup, wearing all white." Plus, her voice was super, super quiet (uh, sexy?) and she was super, super pale—frankly she looked like Casper, the Friendly Ghost. Before my classmates paraded in separately to receive their unique mantra, the teacher stressed that once she gave each of us the word, we should NOT share it with others.

Classmates were going in and out—giggling during their exit. What the hell was everyone finding so funny? Here I was, afraid the teacher would try to convert me and send me to Asia, and there everyone was, walking out as if they saw a cartoon, not a spirit.

It was my turn. The teacher asked me to close the door, and stand in front of her. Then all I remember is her whispering in my ear, "and your mantra is 'ing.'" (Pronounced "eye-ng.") I said, "Excuse me, what did you say?" She repeated, "Your mantra is 'ing.'" "Uhhhh," I stopped, "can I have another mantra because 'ing' sounds like 'boing' and I don't think I will be relaxed repeating that sound...?"

The teacher reminded me that she gave me a special mantra all my own, which proved to me (at the time) that she hated me. Who would give someone a phrase like "blue balls" with a sound like nails on a chalkboard when they're trying to promote inner peace? I was so pissed, and like a naughty detective, I asked my fellow classmates in the parking lot if they cared to share their mantra (even though we were told not to). Sure enough, we all came clean and it is my recollection that this teacher gave us *all* the same mantra! What?!

Yay! She didn't just hate me; *She hated the whole class!* Phew. Seriously, years later, once I shut my mouth and finally matured, I came to realize that whatever word you want to focus on, whether it be "ing" or "flowers," the rhythm—just like the "I am talented and unique" sing-song I shared in Step Four—can be very relaxing and empowering. TM is awesome.

#Choose your sounds wisely when relaxing.

#Sticks and stones can really break your bones.

#Rebooting is medication for your soul.

Look, I told you already I'm not totally a kumbaya kinda guy; however, by signing up for the TM class, I proved I was open to the idea of connecting mind, body, and spirit probably earlier than most of the people who are reading this book. After years of slogging away for others, I realized that no matter how hard I worked, a corporation only cares about its bottom line and office politics: if I didn't unplug and disinvest, I literally was going to shoot myself. I have a few friends that won't enjoy themselves during the week because they say it's a "school night." I find that phrase so unnerving. It's been a long, long time since I've had to go to school, so I really don't know what that means. Is it a way to put our lives on hold? And when it comes to Sunday night, some friends in their fifties, who work in corporate, literally start shaking in anticipation of Monday.

#Turn a manic Monday into a marvelous one.

#Denying sex to your partner because it's a school night will lead them to divorce you.

We cannot work to the max without the power of rebooting from it all—even CEOs everywhere will agree. After we step away and come back, boy, are we refreshed and ready to take on the world with gusto. A coworker and friend of mine named Marjorie at the MTA Data Center gave me a great piece of advice:

#If you work like a workhorse, you will be treated like one.

That's right. You have a right to unplug too. Unless you are Jesus, Buddha or Moses, you should not be expected to give

141

up your weekend to communicate with your bosses. For what? There will always be more work during the week. No one needs to steal your downtime. Is all this chitchat so time-sensitive that it can't wait until normal business hours? After literally sitting in a chair for two years while building a business, I don't care if people think I'm less-than, simply because I won't read every email on the weekend.

#Unless you're a doctor on call, you do not have to be available on any electronic device 24/7.

#*You* will do a better job at work if you step away from the computer more often.

So don't let anyone convince you otherwise...because they are wrong.

I have some friends that must find a remote island without any cell service in order to feel less guilty about taking a vacation. You should *not* have to travel five thousand miles away to feel comfortable unplugging. You should have the right and the power to turn it off when the day is over, so that you can do a better job when the lights come back on.

Take your pulse and think about why you panic when you don't look at your business emails on the weekend. If a boss can take a two-week vacation, it's sad to think that you can't relax and let someone else take over for a while. I don't know why people are so proud of never taking a vacation at work. It's not good for them or the company. Do they really think the boss is going to translate those vacation days into millions and millions of dollars?

#The office went bankrupt before the employee recouped the cash for the vacation days not spent.

So, what do I do for fun? Go out to a dance club in the middle of the week! Yeah, if I do that disco deed during the week, my ass will be dragging in the office; however, I'll be at a focused level of relaxation because I kept my body moving instead of sitting in a seat as if I'm a prune continually shriveling. Another way I decompress is to watch corny TV shows that are so dumb they're great.

#We're all breathing at the same time, going down the conveyor belt of age.

#You cannot do a great job on Monday unless you unplug on Sunday.

Like a plant that needs water and sunlight, we need downtime, nourishment, exercise, and rest. When I started Mouth Public Relations in 2006, I went from my bed to my desk (in the same room) for two years, forgetting to go to the gym or walk because I was obsessed with building my business. Years later, I had to get a fucking hip replacement because, in my non-medical opinion, of all the arthritis built up from being complacent. If only I had understood the power of unplugging and decompressing my guesstimate is that I would not have needed the surgery because I wouldn't have been as stiff as a sculpture.

My uber-awesome sixtysomething friend, Veronica, had a hip replacement and two knee replacements; however, that doesn't stop V from getting out to hike, bike, swim—you name it. V has a husband ten years younger, so she will not let her titanium plates and pins stand in the way of her marriage. It's very easy for someone getting older to stand at the emotional crossroads of their life and make a choice about which road to take. If you make a right, you'll be in a wheelchair by sixty-eight; if you go left, you'll be at the ice rink spinning in a pink tutu.

All kidding aside, it wasn't always roses for Veronica. She was living with constant pain; even after all those joint replacements, she had sciatica that nearly crippled her. She would go to physical therapists, hypnotists—you name it, she would try it. After living with constant dull pain for years, V decided to try acupuncture. Once the needles get to the nerve that's causing the pain, the acupuncturist attaches a mini cable, called "e-stim" (as if it's an electro cable charging a car battery—but in this case, it was electro-stimulating and releasing all the spasms). Within six sessions, Veronica's sciatica was history.

**#Sometimes in order to unplug,
you really need to plug yourself in!**

#Give yourself a jolt of decompression.

Find your own way to decompress. Not everyone reboots by finding solace in the typical definition of relaxation. Write. Listen to music. Go shopping. Renovate and design a property. And go out with the friends who feel they've graduated from the school of adulthood. Whether it's a Sunday or a Wednesday, as I've said throughout this book, we are all on this Earth and time is ticking. We don't breathe differently because it's a school night or because Johnny is twenty-five and Bobby is forty-five.

Jamie's idea of chilling out is buying an apartment, hiring a team to demolish it, and put it back together in a sleek renovation. Annie's way to let loose is going to a museum. Gosh, can you break a sweat letting loose at The Guggenheim? Jordan—who looks more like a football player than a hairdresser—loves, loves, *loves* to bake brownies. Renee watches trashy TV to unwind, and Dereck loves to travel around the world and ride rollercoasters.

#Find solace in your version of meditation.

My friend, Chico, is the most loyal, kind-hearted person I know. His version of rebooting is to work every week at "God's Love We Deliver," a charity whose mission is to improve the health and well-being of men, women and children living with HIV/AIDS, cancer, and other serious illnesses by alleviating hunger and malnutrition. They prepare and deliver nutritious, high-quality meals to people who, because of their illness, are unable to provide or prepare meals for themselves. It's hard to believe that Chico has been chopping carrots and making muffins for the organization for close to twenty years.

#Time flies when you're giving back.

#Giving back gives more back to you than you can imagine.

If you're looking to unplug on a date without going straight to bed, why not suggest that you go to the beach or to the park, put out a blanket, listen to classical music (do you know what that is?), and just chillax? Not every word that includes the letter "x" leads to sex. In this case, going out and unplugging to the sounds of waves dancing to the sounds of Pavarotti leads to one hell of a high note! How refreshing a date like that could be.

#Life happens.

#Take a breath. It's all going to be OK.

How can you possibly get out of your own way when you're tensed up, stressed out, and frazzled? Unplugging and unwinding is absolutely essential—for your sanity, and your life!

While you're seriously pondering the notion of a personal reboot, let's **"TAKE-A-QUIZ"** to make sure you're ready to unwind and let go:

1. **Do you feel guilty taking time off?** No ethical employer will fire you because you're taking vacation or personal days, and want to take off on the weekends or holidays. No matter how good of a job you do, you will not earn tenure simply because you're burning out and working goliath-type hours. Travel should not be only for the rich. Find your dream vacation and save up to make it happen. Have the courage to walk out and turn off so that you can do a more focused job when you return.

2. **Do you have the courage to turn a school day into a "me" day?** Whether it's a Sunday or a Thursday, we're all living and breathing the same way, unless you're having a really bad COPD attack. Our breaths don't change simply because we're at a job—or dare I say, a job we hate. Have the "courage" to stop and take a mental health day in the middle of the week, because you don't get brownie points for dropping dead of exhaustion. Note: if you do drop dead at work, they'll send an assistant to your funeral in conjunction with HR conducting a job search for your replacement!

3. **Do you work out?** A workout can work wonders to help you unplug from *everything* coming at you—emails, social media, calls on the weekend from your boss, texts from your long-lost cousin—and unwind. Look for popular reboots like yoga, Tai Chi, or Pilates—heck, even

walk on a treadmill or spin on a bike. As I learned the hard way, you gotta keep it all moving to live a healthful life. These outlets are guaranteed to make you feel relaxed, renewed, and as flexible as a rubber band while giving you an edge on living longer.

4. **Have you ever meditated?** Whether you choose TM, yoga, or whipping up your favorite pot brownies (the legal ones, that is), find the right technique that lowers your heart rate. If you need some guru-light guidance, log onto a creative visualization podcast or pop in a CD. Oh, and by the way, drinking until you pass out is *not* a form of meditation.

5. **Are you in constant high octane mode?** Take the words "supersized" and "XXL" out of your vocabulary. There's no reason to always be in constant overstimulation. Think of the world as if everything about it is a whole food. Keep it simple, not overprocessed, and you'll be surprised that, just as your taste buds come back when you get off sugar, your feelings will be more sensitive when you lower your controversy intake level.

Breathe.

Step Eight:

Work on Your Work Ethic

I can't stress enough how important working on your work ethic is for getting out of your own way to work in your dream career. Frankly, the issues brought up in this Step concern 99.5 percent of Millennials and Boomers (and those in between) who are seeking employment.

The more Millennials I interview for work, the more it becomes painfully clear that, for the most part, "work ethic" seems to be a lost art. What a sad fact. WTF did "out-placement services" teach kids about how to step up and out after graduation? Are schools afraid the students will throw a hissy fit in protest over the hard work that's needed to compete in the workplace? Where are the parents in this tragedy? Look, I've had my bratty moments as a kid and certainly as a young adult (did I mention I'm a brat sometimes now?), but never, ever, ever, ever would I dare to walk into a job interview or the first day on a new job with entitlement issues. Hardworking parents who care about their kids' future understand there is a strategy, a tactic to get their children employed. If you were a fly on the wall during a job interview, you would cringe at the antics that go on— frankly, these antics are probably why there is even an industry called HR, which flushes out the resumes before they're seen by supervisors. I own and run a small shop with high-profile clientele, so I not only wear the CEO cap, but also oversee the billing and HR stuff—as well as run the staff of account executives. (If these caps were wigs, I would have lots of hair on my head.)

Because there is so much competition vying for the one spot, giving a strong interview and being prepared is paramount.

Imagine when "Johnny" walked into Rhoda's office with headphones plugged into his ears and plopped his butt down in my office as if he was an old friend. Immediately, Rhoda knew something was way off. Rhoda was just in the middle of negotiating a major TV appearance for a client, so Rho didn't have a lotta time to putz around with someone who seemed to have entitlement issues. Like many of the Millennials who walk in for a job, Johnny didn't have a clue as to who he was interviewing with, what he was interviewing for, and why he even wanted a job. When his cover letter only consisted of the following lines, "Please see my resume as I am interested in the position," Rhoda figured that Johnny was desperate for help—even though he thought he was doing Rho a huge favor by gracing her office with his presence.

The strongest asset Johnny had was his personality. The weakest trait he displayed was being unprepared for getting this job. From the way Johnny spoke, it was clear that he hadn't looked at Rhoda's website, and didn't understand the job description advertised. When she asked him what his entry-level salary requirement was, Johnny said, "65K."

Without any experience, and without any interest in understanding what the job at hand entails, smiling Johnny wasn't so happy when he was escorted out of the building. *Next*!!

Millenials aren't the only generation that have "problems" interviewing.

The next candidate was "Thomas." Wow, was he disconnected to the situation at hand—which was uber-surprising, because coming into a job interview for an entry-level position with a resume that exuded fifteen years of experience was a sign of desperation. Steven is a huge proponent for giving anyone a job who really wants to work with him—even if you're overqualified; however, Steve is not here to offer you the position if all you're interested in is the benefits. Talking about benefits within the first five minutes of the interview—when you haven't even substantiated your interest in the gig—is a sign you'll take the job for a few months until the next one comes along. Even though Thomas clearly read that the job was an entry-level position, he tried his best to convince Steven the slot should be elevated to management and that he should be paid more. Typical. Does every candidate understand that companies need to work with budgets and can't just pull a salary out of their ass? Steve would have been more apt to take Thomas seriously if he had humbled himself, had done some due diligence about the specific job for hire, and had done a less than stellar attempt at convincing Steven his version of the job was better than the one that was posted.

Perhaps the reasons for these next excuses stem from the name of my business website, the kind of clients we rep, or the industry of public relations and social media we work in. For the most part, the only frame of reference these kids have for PR comes from MTV, Bravo, and other reality-based television. They watch shows featuring "celebrity" publicists who always seem to be overly concerned about putting on a party or going to a hip-hop concert in the Hamptons rather than focused on getting a solid ROI ("Return on Investment") that sells the client's product.

Trust me, there is more to event planning—which is just a sliver of PR—than ordering hors d'oeuvres for a cocktail reception as reported on reality TV. And not every PR firm works with rappers and fashion brands either. The world is a big place with a lot of products that fall outside the comfort zone of most Millennials—and it seems as if everyone has a handler nowadays. ("Handler" is another name for publicist.) That makes this industry still relevant and sexy, until, that is, the sexy robots invade the Hamptons and take over.

The fresh-out-of-college job candidates who boast they are a member of the PRSA (Public Relations Society of America) and walk in with a resume riddled with typos—not to mention the fact that they have no clue what the major news organizations are—should really give their money back to the organization. Telling a potential employer that you get your daily news from Twitter without telling the employer what news orgs you're following on the platform is a red flag that you're clueless about just how in-depth the daily research required for PR is. Think of it like this: if you're a contractor, you have the necessary tools, such as nails, hammer, wood, level, etc.; if you own a gas station, you own pumps, squeegees, lube, oil, etc. So if you're a publicist, why don't you have a handle on the outlets you need to pitch to?

Here's a story that sums up how clueless people are when their egos gets in the way of their work ethic:

David was a trust fund kid from Westport, CT—who, frankly, didn't need to work—but he was smart enough to know that he needed to do something; being a deadbeat from the Gold Coast was not attractive to potential dates. I'm not sure why David needed to book an Uber every morning to take the hour-plus drive (in traffic) from Westport into NYC. However, with car in tow, it was further perplexing why David was always late.

As you can imagine, David didn't have any real qualities to call himself a publicist. Frankly, hiring him was a favor to a huge literary editor. With a reference like that, it made sense to give David a shot. After all, Sharyn Rosenblum and Jacqueline Deval gave me my shot—why not pay it forward to David?

I personally taught David the ropes—soup to nuts—on how to do my job. It was as if he had been accepted to the Harvard of PR classes. With my encouragement behind him, David was beginning to book credible interviews for our clients.

Even with all my good intentions, David felt it was his right to quit with a day's notice and work for a competitor, in conjunction with trying to steal our clients (who kept asking us why David was soliciting them). Here I was doing a favor for the literary editor, putting my heart and soul into a wannabe publicist, only to get screwed. Here's a reason why business owners develop a hard edge when it comes to doing people favors.

What was interesting to learn, a year later, was that David was flat-out fired by the competitor for trying to convince one of their clients to pay David directly. After a year and a half of experience, David felt he was ready to open his boutique PR firm. The competitor sent me an email saying, "I'm sure you know we hired David— did you know he said he was unemployed at the time we hired him? I'm not sure how you were able to work with him."

#Be careful who you talk to in business.

**#The stories you tell in confidence
always come back to haunt you.**

#Karma is a true bitch.

Getting ready for a job interview is in many ways more important than doing the actual job. You can't blame candidates whose parents don't encourage them to do any research beyond Google about the do's and don'ts of interviewing. And the infamous smartphone is not a great tool for writing a cover letter either—as we read in Johnny's above— because every damn letter I get from a twentysomething looks as if they're posting on Twitter. Speaking of cover letters, it's rare to find any candidate who writes a pitch as to *why they want to work at the company* versus *just needing a job.* You can always tell when a candidate didn't do their homework: in their letter, all they talk about is themselves and not about how interested they are in the opportunity presented. What the candidate doesn't realize is that someone like me *desperately* wants to hire the next person who walks in the room. As the CEO of a business, I don't have time to listen to a weak candidate who isn't prepared. Yeah, I love to read cover letters where the job seeker forgets to globally replace the name of the previous company they applied for. OK, I know that young people must cast a wide job net. However, there is no excuse for having a conversation with a candidate who is clearly misguided about who we are and what we do. If you're looking for a job, there are two questions you need to answer:

1.   Why do you want to work for the company?

2.   Why are you the best candidate for it?

As I mentioned earlier, when twenty- to thirtysomething candidates walk in for a job, some come in flip-flops, ripped jeans and crop tops, most forget to *bring* their resumes (One candidate said to me, "You can print it out because I emailed it to you..."), and at least sixty percent are clueless when it comes to understanding *what* they're interviewing for. If the schools aren't prepping their peeps, the news-breaking story here is the smartphone isn't prepping them either, unless that means clicking onto the company's website—which is a rare exercise, it seems. Hell, I asked someone why they wanted to work at my company, and they said it was because they wanted to work for an architectural PR firm. (Uh, we are not that kind of agency, young man.) The trick questions always seem to be:

1. What clients on our website interest you?

...and then the kicker, which drives newbies back home to mommy:

2. Where do you see yourself in five years?

Truthfully, no one knows!

Please, please, please:

3. Before you go to a job interview, go on the company's website!

If an interviewer asks you where you get your news, it also pays to know the specific trades of the architecture industry if you're looking to work in a PR firm that specializes in representing architects. And yes, they expect you to be on top of the news *every day.* ("Oh, I'm sorry. I didn't know our client was in the *NYT* because I was at a wedding at the Cape this weekend.")

**#If you're working in the service industry,
represent your clients as if they're family members.**

#News doesn't take a holiday.

**#Like a building developer needs plans,
publicists, hairdressers, interior designers,
and many other professionals,
need media and social contacts.**

Let's talk about older job seekers. If you're going to work in PR, or any related field, you've got to be one up with the "new" technology, such as understanding the Internet, blogging, websites, and social media. I wouldn't sound dumb to it all, if I were a sixtysomething person looking to come back to the workplace. It's not attractive and cute to lack the knowledge of the ever-changing industry you're looking to get back into. Plus, before you waste your and the potential employer's time, crunch the numbers you need to make the salary work—keeping in mind that you'll most likely be considered if you're able to work for a competitive salary. If you still reminisce about losing your job at Rubenstein Public Relations, Inc., (a huge PR firm that represents global brands, including the Miss Universe Organization, amongst others), where the salaries might be a third higher, small shops can't afford you. Don't price yourself out of the market, and/or don't go to an interview where you know the salaries will be lower than what you can afford to work for.

#Before an older candidate walks into an interview, they have to turn an employer's preconceived skepticism (about working with overqualified candidates) into an opportunity worth exploring.

#Older Candidates Beware: are you too expensive for the industry you want to stay in or get back into?

People like me understand everyone has a budget and needs to make a salary that allows them to pay bills. If you know the job is at an associate level, please don't send a resume where your last gig was a vice president—unless you can prove to the interviewer that you're here for reasons beyond money.

#Read the job posting and tailor your resume and cover letter to fit the opportunity.

Shaquita lost her job when the smartphone took over her job as assistant for a photo developer company, and she was canned abruptly. She had to get another job ASAP because in two weeks, her rent was due. Desperate for employment, she clicked on every job seeker website she could find, and because her last job was an executive assistant she was able to transfer her skills to a company that owns various newspaper stands across the Northeast. Unfortunately, Shaquita missed a great opportunity because she didn't do her homework before going to the interview. Newsflash to Shaquita: you are probably not going to get your six-figure salary working as an assistant for a mom-and-pop newspaper stand distributor!

If you've spent twenty-five years at another career, your cover letter to an employer has got to be very savvy—making your experience in one industry seamless with another. Again, employers aren't that needy: they really, really want any candidate at any age to show their worth. It doesn't do anyone any good when the candidate talks and talks about experiences that don't pertain to the job at hand—that is, if the story they're telling doesn't lead them to support why their experiences mesh with the position they're interviewing for.

#When interviewing, don't wear yourself out
and talk about subjects that don't pertain to a job.

#An interview isn't a chit-chat with friends.
It is a business meeting.

**#Candidates need to shift the interview
so it's about the company, not solely about them.**

#Employers love to be stroked.

Personally, I owe it to my clients to hire those who are going to do the absolute best for them, seem interested, and most importantly, share a passion to get them a result. Bottom line: if you know what the mission is for the job, you'll prep for a stronger interview.

# # #

Once you get the job, how do you keep it? Let me give you an example from the PR world.

> The Saperstein Brothers, a boutique commercial real-estate company, likes to give new employees a chance. Unfortunately for the brothers, they give newbies way too many "opps" to redeem themselves, even when both the candidate and their executive team concur that the job might be over the head of the new hire. Typically, their approach doesn't work out for either party. If a candidate isn't right for the position, an employer most likely knows it within the first three months the new hire starts. (That's why many companies have a three-month grace period before benefits kick in.) The Sapersteins really should not keep staffers around for months and months on the fantasy that, suddenly, they're going to morph into commercial realtor of the year, which obviously isn't going to happen. Once a new employee gets the

gig, they've got to abide by the rules of the company. In many companies who that sensitive information on their clients, employers ask employees to sign a confidentiality agreement (they can't talk about the business to others outside the company) and a non-compete agreement (they can't steal staffers and clients for two years). What really made one of the brothers turn from nice to nasty was when staffers gossiped about clients to other colleagues—or even to other clients. Imagine if you're a business owner with a certain dollar amount in your budget to spend on your new office space in NYC. You are private, but your mealy-mouthed broker has told everyone, including *The Real Deal* website. Talk about unethical! There is just no place for gossip and office politics when you've agreed to act in confidence.

**#Employees who have their employers' back
are ultimately more valuable.**

**#Never work with friends
unless they are invaluable to your business.**

#A friend who works with you shouldn't steal away clients.

I have three rules for people who work with me (except the other rules, like don't steal, lie, or cheat), and those are:

1. Show up on time.

2. Be relatively friendly.

3. Give it your best.

What does "give it your best" mean? Here's a secret revealed: *always* work two steps ahead of your superior and the customer; anticipate what they're going to ask you before you're asked. That puts out a potential fire of miscommunication, because you've already pre-addressed an issue. If you're hired as an assistant, produce work and have an attitude of someone two steps higher than you up the ladder. Take on more work if you can. Stay later than everyone else. Show that you really care, no complaints. Don't think "sweatshop," think "opportunity." If you're given a deadline and you don't think you're able to meet it, remember that you're a staffer in a business, not a student in college. Unless your boss hears from you, she'll think you're going to get the job done; if you're not, let her do *her* job and find someone to help. No one will ever fault you for communicating clearly and explaining why something has the potential for falling through the cracks.

Do not, and I repeat, "Do N-O-T" step on someone else's toes in the workplace to get ahead. You were put on this Earth to get a tan from the rays of your own sunshine; don't steal from a colleague's hot spot.

#Those who step on others in the workplace are called "backstabbers."

If you foresee a problem that falls under your purview, walk into your boss's office with the solution—not just the problem. Even if you're overwhelmed with the task at hand, take a breath, and think of something. Keep in mind that employers didn't hire you to give them back a homework assignment. That's what we call "delegating up," which is a turn-off to the who-ha who pays the staff's salaries.

#When you work for an employer, look at him as your personal client.

If you can live up to those rules, which I'm hoping you were taught (and this is a refresher course), you're going to be in great shape working with me—or for most other bosses too. In my career, I'm a self-proclaimed Eveready Bunny of Business that doesn't stop...sometimes to the point of obnoxious. To this day, I can work from midnight and beyond—especially if it's a "billing" day. By the end of the shift(s), I'm embarrassed to say there are days when I forget to drink water or eat—it's as if I'm possessed by the ghost of old bosses past who say, "die, fucker; die for your job...." But that's not the case. It's not about pain for me. It's about total productivity and having the power to run the show every day. When you own a business, you must get a job done or else your business tanks. When you work for a business, you must run your own personal show like the boss and show the execs just how valuable you are to the team and the establishment.

#

Let's give one example of work ethic and public relations. It seems as if a lot of people don't know what the hell PR is, so here's a cheat sheet for you to grasp. Unlike hiring an interior designer (where you know you're going to get a couch and some drapes at the end of the engagement), PR is based on an *effort*—no legitimate agency can absolutely guarantee a perfect result. A lot of the job includes booking clients on television, radio, print, online, and social media outlets, so the success of your campaigns are in the hands of others. Unfortunately, "effort" is somewhat forgotten by clients who don't see the results they are dreaming of. Sure, a publicist can put together an amazing launch for a product, but if there's a news-breaking story, like a terrorist attack, weather event, or a sex scandal, a publicist's work dissipates like fairy dust. In most cases, major national shows will not follow a competitor, which means that if you book a client on *60 Minutes*, for example, *Nightline* will not follow, because they both fall under the category of news magazine show.

I remember this as if it was yesterday. It was 2002, and I had the unique opportunity to work with former Colombian presidential candidate Ingrid Betancourt, who published a book called *Until Death Do Us Part: My Struggle to Reclaim Colombia*. I was her American book publicist, in charge of booking TV, radio, and print interviews in New York City and Washington, DC—her last stop before she was tragically kidnapped by the FARC for six years. I remember Ingrid telling me she had about 20 bodyguards when she goes back to Colombia—why was I the ONLY one in America? She hates flying (so do I)—why were we on the shuttle from NYC and DC? I was literally wearing many hats for this author—her publicist, her bodyguard, her comfort. (Trust me, there were no Whitney Houston songs for this definition of what a bodyguard is for a controversial political candidate.)

It was so exhilarating to negotiate and book the first interview for Ingrid's book on *60 Minutes*. When competing shows heard the news, they took their hats out of the ring and passed. So, with only an email in hand confirming CBS wanted the first booking, the publisher banked on a ton of book orders—all based on a meet and greet, and a conversation between the producer and me.

It was very frustrating—and practically ruined Ingrid's entire campaign—when "60" abruptly backed out. According to a conversation I had with one of the producers, Christiane Amanpour (who was on "60" at the time and was slated to interview her), passed because, according to the producer, Ingrid's numbers in the Colombian presidential election weren't high, so the story wasn't as "hot" as they thought. (FYI: Ingrid met with the shows early on—*before she started her campaign in Colombia.* Did anyone inform Ms. Amanpour of that fact when she confirmed her interest in the story?) After hearing the news that we were not going to kick off this campaign on "60," none of the other competitors felt the need to hop on our softer bandwagon.

#If a national show decides to abruptly cancel the interview, your campaign is in jeopardy of tanking.

A few weeks after the campaign—when Ingrid was kidnapped by the FARC in Colombia—I went back to "60" to see if they would consider covering the tragic news to help free her (with a mention of her book, of course), since the story had turned into hard news around the world. The producer came back and said that they'd "probably" assign Morley Safer to the story *after* Ingrid was freed and/or if she became president. It's amazing how this show, which takes pride in making news, was so uninterested this time around.

So, as exciting as the Ingrid tour was, it wasn't that upbeat back at the job. I remember shortly before the tour, during one of my marathon workdays where I was desperately trying to get more media coverage for this woman, one of my colleagues emailed to ask, "Why are people walking in front of your office interviewing for your job?"

Here I was, literally ripping my throat out pitching an internationally-known personality—and doing a great job, I might add—and my boss seemed mired down in office politics. She was a classic backstabber who didn't have the backbone to give me the courtesy of problem-solving her gripe. Since she was put in her role for political reasons rather than her talent, I decided to bypass my boss and her boss too (who I now refer to as the Pigeon Sisters) and go straight to the CEO, asking to be switched out of this dummy supervisor's clutches. I put out the fire and remained at the company for many, many more years, I might add; the Pigeon Sisters were canned shortly thereafter.

#Working in corporate is like surviving in the jungle.

Keep your eyes and ears open to avoid getting eaten by snakes.

Even though "60" played not-so-nice in Betancourt's sandbox, they did an amazing job when they booked my authors, Michael Jordan's *Driven From Within* and Lawrence Taylor's *LT: On the Edge*, on separate occasions. Both campaigns took off like wildfire. In fact, Mike Wallace told me off camera that, after Lawrence Taylor repented over his lack of parenting skills and cried profusely during the taping (some of which appeared in the final cut), he "got more than what he bargained for" that weekend at the Lowe's Hotel in South Beach (where the interview was filmed). That one segment made Lawrence Taylor's book a *NYT* best-seller, and also gave Taylor's manager, Mark Lepselter, his first national TV show. Lepselter apparently got way too big to ever return my calls or emails after that (even though I was the one who negotiated that interview), but HarperCollins (the publisher of Taylor's book and Ingrid's too) gave me an "A" for this campaign—that's what really mattered.

#All is forgiven, 60 Minutes!

#A publicist is only as good as the clients they represent.

**#If it weren't for a publicist,
most great interviews would have never been booked.**

# # #

Having a solid work ethic will help you bypass your competition as you move up the ladder and stay employed. I hope these examples of how to get a job, how to keep a job, how to avoid the backstabbers in a job, and how to be one step ahead in your job (as well as a few backroom antics of my job) have helped you to understand how the working game works. Are you ready to **"TAKE-A-QUIZ"** about work ethic and how to prep for a job opportunity?:

1. **How much prep time do you take for a job interview?** If your answer is "not much," it's time to realize that prepping for an interview is important to making the ultimate first impression because you will exude confidence. Think of yourself as a guest on "The Tonight Show" with Jimmy Fallon. Without apology, talk about yourself and make the case for why you're the perfect candidate, and extrapolate on the company's mission statement, and job philosophy, for example. (You'll get a lot of info from their website.) Remember, employers don't want to be the "Eveready Battery of Job Interviewers," they are praying that *you* will be the candidate. In your prep, figure out what excites you about the position. Don't simply appear as if you're just anxious to get any old job. And for God's sake, don't answer a potential employer with one word answers, and don't come into the interview looking like you've just had sex.

2. **Are you jealous of co-workers and spend your time focused on other peoples' jobs and not yours?** Keep the office politics and the jealousy at home. Do *not* spend your time dismantling other colleagues' jobs even if you know they're unqualified. If you don't like working in the environment, get out and go to a healthier place. And do not screw someone to get ahead. It's bad karma.

3. **Once you get the position (congrats!), do you show up for your job on time, be relatively friendly and try your best?** If you've got that covered and you make a mistake, no one will ever fault you. Be

conscious of letting your supervisor know when you're overwhelmed, so that he can help you navigate the item at hand, or even get someone to help. Team effort!

4. **Are you ready to offer a solution when there's a problem?** Employers don't have all the answers. Before you walk into your boss's office with a problem, invest some research and thought into solving it. Show your worth to your supervisors by coming in with action items that move beyond a crisis. Prove how valuable you are to the company and how you have your boss's back.

5. **Do you give proper notice when you leave a job?** It's customary to give an employer at least two weeks' notice so that you can wrap up the necessary items at hand and your employer can find a replacement. Some staffers stay longer if needed. Exit a job as if you're just beginning it. It's important to make sure your boss and your coworkers have a grasp on where they need to pick up where you've left off. Prepare an exit document and really help your soon-to-be former employer make sure the transition runs smoothly. You never know where people end up: the assistant that's here today might be the CEO at a job you're looking for later. And the boss yesterday might be called by your potential employer without you even knowing it. Don't fuck them over.

As long as you look up at the opportunities that are put in front of you—whether they fall under your expertise or not—like my surprising career in PR—you're going to embark or continue on the wonderful journey of work. If you love your job, the work ethic you need to abide by should not only be second nature but a pleasure to live up to because you want your company to succeed. If you hate what you're doing, have the courage to get out of your own way and get out. There is bound to be something that will rock your world. You deserve to be happy.

Step Nine:

Shift Gears

Unlike a car where you can literally shift a gear from reverse to drive, when you shift emotional gears, it's understandable you might totally freak out—because to many, change (voluntary or involuntary) really hurts. Shifting gears can be thrilling or so painful while it's unravelling before us. Some people volunteer to make changes. For instance, I like to move from home to home—state to city to country. It's not as if I'm dodging tax payments or anything; however, I find shaking up my scenery very exciting, while others get emotionally upset with the fact they have to leave their nest. For me, shifting that gear is so much fun: "Sign me up!"

Yesinia agrees—she doesn't blink when it's time to move. She is a star prosecutor, and seems to sail through the court system, winning every case she's in charge of. In fact, weeks after a high-profile trial was decided upon (in Yesinia's favor), the defending attorney was so impressed with her professionalism that he offered Yesinia a job to head up a branch of the firm in LA, three thousand miles away from her home.

Within six weeks, Yesinia put her condo on the market in NYC, and put down roots in Bel Air, Cali. She bought a car, chose the perfect office for the West Coast branch of the law firm, and started representing clients. A week after Yesinia won her first trial, her aunt came to visit her in her new home. It was only after she finally sat down to relax that Yesinia realized she accomplished "all that" in such a short amount of time.

#If you love what you do, time is your friend.

Here's an opposite example of change, where you don't sign up for it.

> Robert didn't want his kids to have a backyard pool. He knew his wife, Stacey, wasn't detail-focused enough to watch over the children like a hawk, especially when they were darting in and out of the water. Needless to say, Stacey was so obsessed with keeping up with The Friggen' Joneses, and Robert was intent on making Stacey happy. "If the neighbors have a pool, we must get one too," Stacey kept saying—until they got one. Did this woman star in *Nightmare on Elm Street* or what?
>
> It's great for some to have the luxury of swimming in your back yard; however, not every family with boys and girls under the age of ten should purchase one—so I'm told.
>
> No one predicted that Bobby, Jr., the six-year-old son of the couple, would slip on the diving board and break his neck. This was the first death in the young family. No one should go through what these poor people experienced, even though the dream that Stacey wanted went against Robert's intuition. I'm sure you know the saying, "no parent wants to bury their child." It was tragic to attend the funeral.
>
> Gear switch: The week after the funeral, the pool was filled in and Robert filed for divorce. He got full custody

of the surviving children because Stacey admitted to having an affair and leaving the kids home alone with the same neighbor she was competing with.

This scenario was, indeed, emotionally tragic and disturbing; it's something no one could prepare for. Life happens, sometimes forcing us to switch into gears we didn't know we had in the first place. Perhaps Robert's abrupt 180-degree turn was a way to bury wounds that didn't have time to heal. I wasn't around to hear what happened, and I wish him peace.

Now let's shift gears and talk business.

As I've hinted throughout the book, like a trash bag full of garbage, older people are being tossed out, replaced, and branded as irrelevant to society. It's tragic to think that we all sit back and just let people in high places put us out to pasture, as if we're a cow.

Big Brother is bullying us into thinking that an ageless robot (even one with a sweet voice like Siri or Alexa) can take the place of us humans. The first ones to be replaced are the Boomers. I understand when young ideas take over antiquated strategies, but I strongly disagree with the idea that a machine is going replace us—whatever age we are. What's even crazier: some people in their late twenties think they're washed-up too and ready to be sold on the clearance rack.

#If you think you're well-done, it's time to tenderize.

#Bring back humanity.

If you're one of those glass-half-empty types thinking your days with your employer are numbered, I just want to remind you that I started a whole new career (in publishing) at thirty-three. Shifting gears again, in middle age, I started my own boutique PR business at forty-eight, and rebranded it as a PR/social media firm at fifty-eight. I'm not rolling in the dough, but I'm certainly sustainable and keeping a staff employed in The Big Apple, better known as "way-too-expensive NYC." Honestly, it's not because I am a super talent—I have a big mouth, I invest in preparation, am open to possibilities and seize opportunities without overanalyzing.

#Having the flexibility and self-awareness to know when it's time to shift gears will help make you happier and more productive.

Vince is an example of someone who is stuck in "neutral," and is a walking time bomb of negativity. He really didn't like what he did for a living any longer, but instead of making a change, his new job was to complain—that way, he was occupied with something that he could control. He couldn't control the fact he was the oldest one standing at the job; he couldn't control that he was getting older. He could control getting out of his own way, for sure, and shaking his life up. However, he chose to complain because behind all that was fear and laziness.

When Vince complains to me, it's as if he just wants to

rant—forgetting I'm five years older (and just maybe a little wiser) than he is. If he would take the time to see that he could live it up on his own terms, he'd jump at the chance to change up his "nightclub act" and write a new script.

In my dreams, I want to say, "For God's sake, Vince, get up off your ass, out of your negative persona, and please stop complaining, making more and more excuses that exhaust you...and me! Tell it to your therapist, dude. The same complaints are boring; I want to rip my hair out." (Oh wait, I have none.) "You've whined about the same issues for the last ten years, you're really showing more signs of laziness than you have of concern." What Vince doesn't understand is that he's still the best in his field, with a savvy sense of confidence that many admire. However, his bad attitude is what people *know him for*. What a waste.

**#If you aren't interested in shifting gears
and get stuck in the middle of the road,
you're not only in your own way, but in everyone else's.**

**#If you hate your job that much,
make the effort to find another one.**

**#You will never know
there's a great opportunity ahead
unless you put yourself out there.**

Shifting gears can be scary for some, because they think they've done something wrong in need of fixing, and they're either lazy or just plain scared.

#Your job could be old and outdated—not you!

#Let the universe bring on opportunity.

#Survival is a social skill.

We've heard Vince's obstacles—something that he could take control of and make the shift; however, not everything that pertains to shifting gears has to do with changing jobs, or family tragedy.

What about love?

Angelo was with his boyfriend two years too many. The boyfriend was cheating, and Angelo was miserable, not believing that there was any way out. He made less money than the cheater, and thought he couldn't afford living on his own. That's when his friends at the gay chorus came to the rescue! Through networking, Angelo found a new roommate through a friend of a friend at the organization—a flight attendant who never was home because of his crazy schedule. Even though Angelo was closing one door, a new one flew open—a perfect scenario, in fact, because it was as if he had the apartment to himself, without paying the entire rent!

I heard about Jeanette's story from a friend who works with abused women.

Jeanette loved wearing short skirts and very high, pointy shoes, even if she had circulatory problems where her feet seemed to be bursting out of her pumps. Jeanette's style consisted of bold colors and patterns—yellow and red polka-dot skirts, green baseball caps with a pink sweatshirt...you name it, Jeanette wore it, even though the style didn't flatter her body type.

My friend told me that Jeanette wore these outrageous outfits because she wanted your eye to deflect away from the bruises on her face. Jeanette confessed that even though she loved her husband so much because they were high school sweethearts, he beat her once a month—after he got his paycheck. After my friend counseled Jeanette, helping her realize there is no place for abusive behavior, Jeanette was ready for a big change that had nothing to do with her abuser. Even though Jeanette admitted she was scared shitless she would end up alone, taking control of her life was much more important to her than living in this hell.

Jeanette was over living with boxes of concealers and other tricks of the trade to hide her welts. Frankly, she was tired of being beaten. Even though she had accepted her role as victim, she didn't want to continue in this storyline any longer, and one day she walked out. With the help of her oldest son, she just left the home she'd lived in for more than thirty years with an overnight bag—no goodbye note—ecstatic and scared to start her life all over again. Two years after her departure, and after divorcing her husband (who ended up in jail for not paying a slew of back taxes—imagine that), Jeanette was out and about...*and dating* her daughter's boss, a widower who, like Jeanette, was looking for a kind-hearted companion.

Reinvention doesn't only pertain to people. What the hell happened to Wang? Remember the Wang Word Processor I spoke about?...the one I worked on at the MTA to pay the rent while pursuing a career in music? What happened to the Sony Walkman? Why didn't Sony shift gears and invent the iPod? Why didn't BlackBerry get out of their own way and create a better version of the iPhone or Android? Why didn't Ringling Brothers reinvent the circus? In Spring 2017, after 146 years in business, the "World's Greatest Show" marked its final performance. Why didn't they become Cirque du Ringling before Cirque du Soleil did?!

**#People and companies
who don't keep their eye on reinvention will crumble.**

Just how do you become relevant (again)?

It's ridiculous for your head to be so deep in the sand you can't see that communicating on the Internet is one of the ways of life. As you've read throughout this book, I've been very critical with how the smartphone is clogging up our lives—but you will never hear me say that it should be eradicated. Look, the whole damn thing isn't going away. You've got to get with the program! It's all about *balance*.

#If you spend too much time on Apple products, do you turn into a foodaholic?

Right now, all the electro-philes are forever excited about the different watches, smartphones, tablets—all the electronic toys they own—but trust me, soon it will be time for the next Apple. If Apple keeps up its passive-aggressive arrogance, it's only a matter of time when their attitude toward the consumer will do them in—no matter how iconic Steve Jobs was. I would be thrilled if a company like Apple would establish a department called "Real Life Experience (RLE)," where everyday people can give Apple pointers on what is right and wrong with their product!

#Wake up. We're all replaceable.

#Making a 180-degree turn in life isn't as scary as Linda Blair's 360-degree head turn in *The Exorcist*!

If you're ready to shift your gears, or still in denial that something's up, why don't you **"TAKE-A-QUIZ"** to help determine what your next steps could be:

1. **What's your strategy to shift gears and reinvent yourself?** Like the four seasons, change is a glorious impetus to keeping yourself relevant. Reinventing yourself can be easily attainable if you have clear goals,

role models of those who you aspire to become, and an
action plan.

2. **Do you confuse arrogance with self-confidence?**
If so, get it straight! Arrogance can hurt you. The more
arrogant you are about yourself, the more people want to
dismember you. People don't want to be around a prick,
so curb your snobbiness and change it up by trying a
little humility.

3. **Do you promote yourself and let people know
you're looking for a new opportunity?** Whether you
are looking for a job, looking for a soulmate, or looking
for just about anything, people aren't mind-readers.
Network, and let people know you're seeking to shift
gears, and open to all possibilities that are put in front
of you.

4. **Are you ready for change?** Telling people you're
looking is just a start. It's all about an action plan to help
you get up and out and start looking. It's always a better
strategy to interview for a job while you have one so that
it doesn't send a message you're desperate. And if you've
been in that relationship way too long and you know it's
gone south, give your partner the courtesy of knowing
it's time for a break—don't just stay in a bad relationship
and cheat.

5. **Is your fear of ageism getting in the way of
shifting your gears?** As you get older, your rich life
experiences really define you, and truly separate you
from others—no matter what age you are. Try focusing on

what makes you extraordinary, homing in on your unique take on the subject at hand that will wow employers to consider you.

If, after you've read this step, you're still clueless, here's some immediate "news you can use" on the job front: Transitioning in your job will be easier if you get up off your ass and get educated with the latest assets that people who work in your field (or a field you aspire to work in), need, in order to stay relevant. I know in work and in life, it's not easy to make changes, even if most of the time, it's not life-threatening. Imagine being the sole breadwinner who has just been diagnosed with incurable cancer and now must make a huge life change and find a permanent home for her kids?

Is your reason for change that drastic? I hope not. Please put change in perspective.

Universally, make sure that, first and foremost, you're open to the idea of change on all levels. Face the fact: if you don't make the turn sooner or later, you'll be stuck in reverse—without a way outta Dodge.

Step Ten:

Rule Your Planet

When I got the news that I was assigned to work with Reverend Bernice A. King (Martin Luther King, Jr. and Coretta Scott King's youngest daughter) for *Hard Questions, Heart Answers,* I could have pinched myself. Here was an opportunity to work with someone from a great, spiritual family—who I was positive would be open to working with me on her project. Uh, not really—even with the news I had locked in *People* magazine (possible front cover), CBS *Sunday Morning,* and *Oprah!*

When the producer of the CBS show called me and asked whether I knew why Bernice had canceled the segment, I was taken aback. In fact, I was shocked and confused—and so was the publishing team at Broadway Books. The opportunity of a lifetime—to be on the premier TV morning news magazine show that sells a lot of product—had turned to dust.

And more cancellations followed. It seemed as if Bernice's office didn't "trust" the strategy the publisher put forth and didn't want to be exploited. Although I wasn't privy to backroom conversations, I do remember the book was releasing while it was publicly reported that CBS and MLK, Jr.'s estate were in dispute over the use of King's "I Have a Dream" speech. Not great timing? Not sure.

In my opinion, Bernice didn't trust her publisher. Even though I was the hired lackey, the team, headed by the very talented publisher, Bill Shinker, allowed me to reach out to Bernice and help her understand that she was giving up an opportunity of a lifetime. After all, the last time I checked, my name wasn't listed as author of *Hard Questions,* so I had nothing to lose but to speak the truth.

The call went stupendously; Bernice was as lovely as she could be. We were able to resurrect most of her PR campaign...and then there were three distinctive moments that made a lasting impression on me. Frankly, moments like these, though few and far between, are one of the reasons why I'm still in the business of public relations.

The first was hearing Bernice lift up, look out, and inspire people at a book signing we planned at the Abyssinian Baptist Church in Harlem. *Wow.* To see Bernice go from "soft-spoken" to "move mountains" when she spoke was extraordinary. The second was when Bernice and I were in the car—and her mobile phone rang. Right when the conversation was over, Bernice turned to me and said, "My mom would like to thank you for taking care of me on this tour." *Wow again.* I'm sure you understand how it felt speaking to Coretta—and hear the word "Thanks," no doubt. And the third, something I will never, ever forget, was when Bernice asked me, later in the tour, to see if we could set up a book signing event in Memphis, the city where her father was assassinated. I recall she said that she'd never been to Memphis. Asking me to coordinate an event in a market that obviously had a lot of moving parts, both emotionally and physically for Bernice, was a sign that she trusted me. It was also a sign she could get out of her own way of distrust and make the experience of sharing the book she had written, and traveling to promote it, more meaningful for her, her audience, and me.

#Trusting someone allows them and you to open your hearts to one another.

#Trusting yourself is the key to ruling your planet.

Ironically, years and years later, I was hired by another publisher to represent James Larry Ray, the brother of MLK, Jr.'s assassin. Talking about gaining experience from all sides of the spectrum—very complicated.

Jonathan was a therapist known for his work with specially-abled children. If you saw this man walk down the street you would never have guessed he helped thousands and thousands of families place their dear siblings into assisted living facilities where the kid's felt safe and protected. Jonathan was considered a God in his circle; however, he had absolutely no self-esteem. In fact, it was perplexing how a man who had virtually no social skills ruled his own planet and had such tremendous strength to change the lives of others. When he approached me to help him promote his book, he really wasn't prepared; frankly, he was a total walking disaster. His book, on the other hand, displayed a powerful persona of its own, which contradicted the one on the other side of the phone, timidly asking for opinions and help in marketing. My advice to Jonathan was to figure out a way to get over his deep-seated wall of shyness and try to envision himself as a "character" in his own book. After all, if you're writing a book that could potentially help millions of more families grapple with the challenges of handicapped children and the funding nightmares that go along with their housing, you've got to have some sort of confidence, wouldn't you think? Here I was, a college dropout with a resume filled with singing techno-pop, helping a Brainiac (and a therapist, no less) overcome his fear. It didn't take long before Jonathan stepped out of his shell and started moving audiences—with the same verve he displayed in his writing.

Totally unrelated, but eye-opening for me: I remember working with the great publisher, Dan Halpern of Ecco, an imprint (at the time I worked with him) of HarperCollins. I remember being assigned a project that was penned by one of the greatest thinkers of our lifetime. The writing was super-smart and very dense. Despite Dan's faith in me, I doubted whether I had the education and smarts to run this campaign. Walking into Dan's office was nerve-racking, because I was going in there to admit defeat before getting started. Ethically, I felt it was important to let Dan know that the guy he hired to run his publicity department wasn't the best guy to run with this tome of a book by a superstar thinker.

After my confession to Dan, he went silent, took a beat, and said, "Justin, none of my smart authors don't give a fuck whether you graduated college. They all want *you* to get them on Oprah!" Wowsa. I just got a stamp of approval to be me, from the guy who trusted I could make things happen for his author peeps. After hearing that Dan valued my talent and street-savvy sensibility, my insecurity shifted. I was ready to get out of my own way and rule not only my planets, but many, many for Dan and others at HarperCollins.

As you're nearing the end of the book, I'd like to dive deeper in my story as a pop-recording artist in the UK, which I left off around the time I was to report back to Heathrow, under orders to leave the country because of the work permit glitch.

Because I wasn't a criminal, the agents allowed me seven days' entry back into London to pack up—though not before they confiscated my passport—and ordered me to promptly report back to the same desk. During this unexpected last leg in London, I saw my spirit go from quasi-star-like to loser, seeing my "chance" of living a life full of creativity disintegrate before my very eyes. With suitcases in hand, I reported back to "that desk" at Heathrow and was quickly (and surprisingly) whisked away to a holding tank, where the likes of suspicious characters from the movie *Midnight Express* were waiting to be expelled from the country like me...or had the English government hired them to kill me?

#If you see an evil eye, shut yours.

#Where is New Jersey when you need it?

When it was time to board the plane, I was escorted by a few bobbies (British slang for "cops"), who put me in a barred paddy wagon that drove right onto the tarmac and right up to the plane. I remember sitting down in coach and feeling like an immigrant who wasn't welcome any longer—just another American criminal, caught and ousted. Here I was, a guy who never smoked a cigarette, smoked a joint, or took drugs, being ejected for a working permit glitch for touring as an opening act. It was only after the plane took off and was wheels-up that the flight attendant gave me my passport back.

Within the few hour flight across the pond, I felt as if I was rewinding my tape: I had left as a musician and was entering JFK as a starving (not even) artist. For the next six months, I fell into a deep depression and literally couldn't speak. (Imagine if I called my company "depression digital" instead of mouth?) In sync with the plane's touchdown was Rock Hudson's announcement that he was diagnosed with AIDS— and it seemed as if *everyone* in New York City had received the same diagnosis. OK, not everyone, but enough for me to feel as if life was over as we all knew it and uncontrollable. WTF was AIDS anyway? I landed in a city that I didn't know any longer—and a world where I didn't understand what the hell was happening.

**#I entered the real Armageddon
and wondered if God was going to punish me too.**

Living back with mom and stepdad Tony during this period was very hard—not because they weren't gracious, and not because I didn't want to be with family. After all, I left home the day after high school graduation...about seven years before this deeply tragic debacle. A lot of my friends were in theatre, some of whom were on Broadway—originals in *A Chorus Line, La Cage Aux Folles, Evita, Dancin', Pippin*—the best of the best was all in New York and blocks away from where I and my family lived. Now, many were dealing with this horrible, incurable illness. If so many artists were rapidly afflicted with this illness, in my mind, I was just a few days before getting a diagnosis too.

At the time when the AIDS epidemic blew up in NYC, from my musical vantage point, it was virtually unheard of in the UK. Like many of my British friends, I was naïve to the whole health scare. It wasn't something people were talking about in London.

Even though I didn't speak at home, I took on a role of a knight in shining armor and became my friends' cheerleader, ruling everyone else's planet (except my own), offering inspiration and hope to all my friends diagnosed with AIDS—while their family members basically disowned them simply because the disease was airborne and infectious. In those days, people wouldn't eat off of dishes and glasses in restaurants simply because that gays had eaten off of them.

I remember when my uber-successful Broadway dancer friend Marc asked me to come to his fancy Central Park West co-op and co-sign his will ("because there was no one else"). As I was sitting there listening to him telling the attorney he was giving the piano to this one, the silver to that one, it suddenly occurred to me that he wasn't giving me anything. Trust me when I tell you, I didn't need anything, nor did I have any place to put a baby grand piano. However, the fact that I was sitting in his home and helping him when no one else would—I thought would put me on his personal "A" list. I was hurt that I wasn't considered "special" enough to make this list. After all, I'm a people pleaser who, for the most part, only wants to be liked.

Even my hyper-sensitivity didn't mask the fact that Marc tossed me out on the street when he didn't need me any longer. As Marc was wrapping up his estate, I made a conscious effort to wrap up my friendship with Marc too. Call me heartless and a prick: while I was at his home being dissed, I decided to get rid of *everyone* I knew that I couldn't count on. It was an eye-opening moment that I had never experienced before: letting people go. You might be thinking: how could I compare Marc's bout with AIDS with my lack of trinkets from his personal collection? Well, not once during my entire time in England, from my arrival through to when I started making a musical name for myself—not to mention my disastrous, embarrassing departure—had Marc ever reached out and supported me. That meeting with Marc, and his attorney, changed my life forever. As I ended my friendship with him and other self-centered acquaintances, I also hung my armor and gave up my knighthood. Ending friendships when the friendship is over was the beginning of me swimming away from my pool of depression. I was organically getting out of my own driver's seat and—without realizing it—starting to become a pilot who rules his own planet.

#Letting go of friends is as necessary as putting a period at the end of a sentence.

#Putting your needs second clogs up your mission to move your life forward.

#You have the power to rule your planet.

# # #

Back at mom and Tony's crash pad that evening was pretty chill. I did *not* share my experiences with Marc or my fears of coming down with AIDS. However, my mom knew something was "brewing" inside of her "kinda was-a should-a been-a pop-star" son. Later on that night, she and I were watching a popular TV news magazine program where we learned about this antidepressant called Xanax. The reporter interviewed a psychiatrist who was using the drug on his patients for the first time. If it was good enough to be featured on TV, it was good enough for her kid, so Elayne thought. What did my mom do next? She called the psychiatrist who was on the show, and asked him to see me. We schlepped from NYC to Morristown, New Jersey and entered a noticeably makeshift office—in fact, an almost vacant space—with one desk in it. I walked in, and without any of the analytical fanfare that comes with meeting a psychiatrist for the first time (I've been to two of them, so I have a minor vantage point), I was handed, without any evaluation or diagnosis, a prescription for Xanax. Before I knew it, my mom and I were sitting in traffic on the Helix interchange going into the Lincoln Tunnel—and I was losing it.

#If you have a nervous breakdown, have it near a hospital and not in traffic going into the tunnel.

The postmortem of losing my big step to stardom, coupled with the loss of friends from AIDS, the decision to let go of friends, and a weight gain from 150 to close to 300 pounds, finally hit me like a rocket ship. Not because I was guilty about ever sharing a word of my fears with my family; it was the fact that I didn't talk and let out some emotional steam. Not being able to express any kind of emotion that allows our fears and our expectations to slip into normalcy was like a pot of boiling water inside my head, and I was ready to explode. I felt deeply flawed and desperate—and terrified. It all came out in the form of uncontrollable crying, right in the middle lane near the tollbooth. Not that attractive at twenty-six.

My mom didn't ask me to stop the tears. She waited until my sobbing subsided until she broke the silence. She said very quietly, and lovingly, "I know why you're depressed. You are gay, and you think you're dying of AIDS."

Huh? Was my mom a psychic? Did I just call-in to the Psychic Friends Network, hosted by Dionne Warwick? Did my mom just *out* me? Phew. OK, so 'yes,' I did think I was dying from AIDS; but getting outed by my mom was one discussion I didn't have to rehearse for *any longer*!

The truth was, it wasn't so much about the gay thing that drove me over the edge. I was dying of *fear* that my mom (and Tony, and my dad, and anyone else whom I knew) was going to disown me for being gay, especially if I was *dying of AIDS*— which, as luck had it, I wasn't. I was so stuck in my own fearful way, it was as if I was being swallowed up by the streets and highways of my mind and buried in an earthquake—along with the techno-pop recording contract that was terminated back in London.

My mom's words, not an antidepressant drug, were the impetus to my recovery from losing my dream in England and for

accepting myself as I am. This discussion ignited the healing I
needed to do to begin to shift gears, reinvent, and start to rule
my planet once again.

**#Moments in life give you strength to *rule your planet*
and find the next "it" that makes you tick.**

**#Sticks and stones do break your bones;
and the power of words can heal (or hurt) you.**

# # #

The psychiatrist my mom found wasn't the only expert she
reached out to from television. Get this: after my mom outed
me, she asked if I wanted to speak with someone about my
sexuality; and who did she suggest? Why, none other than the
fabulous Dr. Ruth Westheimer from *The Dr. Ruth Show*! That's
right, I was a patient of Dr. Ruth's—albeit for a few sessions.
I loved those chats, and I loved feeling more confident in my
choices for sure—even if I flung a cup of coffee (by accident) all
over Dr. Ruth's white rug in her office. *That* was the only regret
going to see the doctor!

Because of ballsy and beautiful Elayne, and the extraordinary
Tony, I was saved from the demons of myself. I was ready to
get out of my own way, get out of their apartment (thank you
to dear Tony for even allowing me to impede on his marriage),
and start to live again. (It's a shame that my twenties were so
hard and tumultuous for me and, frankly, everyone else dealing
with me on all levels.)

My mom and Tony weren't alone in offering understanding and support during my very tumultuous time navigating gay life during the AIDS crisis. But with every story—there's a potential twist that allows one to move their life further into a light that even they don't know is in front of them.

Years later, shortly after the news my biological "Florida" dad was diagnosed with cancer of the liver and pancreas, I had just a few moments alone with him in NYC while he was staying at the Helmsley Medical Tower across from Memorial Sloan Kettering Cancer Center—waiting to be seen by a specialist. It was just weeks before he passed—when he said, "I just want you to know that I know you're gay, and I'm okay with that." Wow. Another family member who gave me a break—gave me more closure that I'm not going to be a walking embarrassment, and I'm not going to be shamed or disowned! Maybe that sqeaky, girly voice as a kid was everyone's wakeup call that Fat Larry was *not* going to marry Miss Vanchieri after all?

Perhaps.

However, it was tragic that after his death, I learned that his second wife and her daughter had stolen my inheritance because my dad's will abruptly changed right after his death— and apparently, his wife's daughter was now the executor. Hmmmmm. My grandfather owned some of the land Lincoln Center was built on, and it seemed as if everyone on my dad's side of the family was clamoring to take what they thought was theirs—even if *theirs* was partly *mine*. The fact was, it wasn't even the question of the money that devastated me—I was absolutely crushed that the estate bullshit that I went through

with David, way back when the *plane landed from London,*
was rearing its ugly head once more and happening again—
*and now with m*y own blood! Here I was again, a purported
second-class citizen to my dad's side of the family? What a
clusterfuck, and what a way for a man and his *only* biological
child to end a relationship. His wife and her daughter did
not have the class to do the right thing—they were always so
desperate to fit in—and I took it all in retrospect, looked up to
the sky, thanked my God that I had the emotional support of
my mom and Tony right by my side—and let go of the nasty,
disgusting antics of my biological dad's wife, her daughter, and
his side of the family.

From that day forward, I ruled my planet the way my planet
needed to spin around the universe.

**#There is no break for commercials
when the big moments in life come before you.**

#Do it boldly.

Through Elayne and Tony's support and spirit—during the
whole gay thing, and during the whole inheritance thing,
I was able to get out of my own way, and really look at my
life as a bigger basket of opportunities. Sure, I have a great
singing voice, I bring an interesting twist to music, and people
bought my records. Sure, I have a great gift for the PR side of
communication, and I've used these skills to my advantage
and have become the top of my game; however, if it wasn't for
the painful journey of letting old doors close (in life and with

friends and relatives) and new ones fling wide open, I would not have been able to take the journey which I am still on.

#Tomorrow isn't guaranteed.

Lynn was a beautiful French-Canadian dancer who somehow became Allen's roommate. At the age of eighteen, Lynn made a six-figure salary by starting dance studios in her country—something that filled a void in a region where there seemed to be a lot of talented kids. Even though Lynn was young, she had an old, nurturing soul and a heart of gold. Hell, Lynn desperately tried to get Allen hired for his first Broadway show ("The Little Prince"), but the deal was he had to lift a girl dancer up and spin her in the air, something he couldn't maneuver because in those days he had no muscle tone. Lost opportunity.

Lynn was a rising star, a ballroom champion, a Broadway dancer, and a married woman (to a guy who was equally as talented—you could see him in the Michael Jackson "Beat It" music video). As great as their lives were, they were equally as tragic. Abruptly, Lynn was diagnosed with a brain tumor and her husband was diagnosed with AIDS—catching the disease from a blood transfusion.

At thirty, and only a few months apart, Lynn and her husband passed away. Two lovebirds and angels steeped in the creative spirit, who, even though were here for a short time, ruled their own planets as if they were on Earth for decades and decades.

**#No matter how old you are,
today really can be the first day of the rest of your life—
if you live it.**

Because of the experiences in my life, I had no other choice
but to shift gears (more times than I knew I was capable of)
when the trip I was taking was clearly going towards the wrong
path, and move out of my own way, without overanalyzing and
wallowing in self-sabotage. When you're encouraged to dream
big, the notion of going high and wide should never be looked
on as foolish or a sin. I had wasted so much time in fear and
guilt, thinking I ruined my life because I didn't go to college,
thinking I had a tragic illness when all I needed to do was go to
the doctor and get checked out, and worrying I didn't fit in the
entire Universe because I didn't' look or act like the Friggen'
Joneses. Finally, I came to realize that my life experiences in
Europe—standing and commanding attention while performing
on some of the most prestigious stages of the world, without
getting a glass beer bottle thrown at me once(!)—were
absolutely and unequivocally my education—an added value to
co-workers, friends, and corporations.

Even though my planet seemed to go through a metamorphosis
as if it was a piece of Silly Putty that wanted to change its
shape and form—almost on a daily basis—I have learned to
pilot my life as if it was that putty toy: although it's manmade, just silicone polymers, my life does, at times, exude an
unusual, extraterrestrial, physical property. It can bounce, and
it certainly can break; but when given a sharp blow, it can also
flow like a liquid.

#My life. Like Silly Putty.

**#Every day that you're here
is the first moment of your life that matters.**

There are so many planets and stars in the galaxy—isn't it time you clicked onto www.starregistry.com and bought one in *your name*? You, like a star, are going on a journey that revolves around something. We know Earth circles the sun...do you revolve around fear or guilt? If you think about it, you've probably had fleeting superstar moments like me when your meteor rises, and some experiences when your planet implodes into the sea. Some of you grab opportunities, some shy away.

That's life, people.

There's no secret to it except having the courage to rule your life as if it's part of an amazing constellation that shines— without apology—very bright! And without living a life ruled by The Friggen' Joneses. I hope some snippets of my stories and examples make the case that we really can sum ourselves up in one sitting, without fanfare. The journey we take can be steeped in a lotta fun along the way too—as long as we are willing to open our eyes and see what's here and what's possible for us in the future. I can assure you that you have the stories inside you that are just waiting to come out. My advice is to have the courage to send it out and let the experience help you grow. We all have that book inside us, and it's your turn to pull the chapters out of your life and give people the gift of knowing you.

Take this last **"TAKE-A-QUIZ"** so that I can rest easy, knowing you're on the right path:

1. **Are you afraid to take "center stage?"** If someone is giving you the gift of "a chance," dive into the opportunity and never worry about the fear of it failing. The stage is yours for a reason. If you doubt why you've been given the chance, you'll never enjoy the journey.

2. **Who needs friends and relatives who don't acknowledge your worth?** There are so many people in the world—do you really need to waste time with those who place you on their "B" list? You will not go to hell if you let go of people, including blood relatives, who don't have your best interest. Remember, it's *your* interest that needs to be fed, not the other way around.

3. **Do you believe your life will incorporate numerous journeys and possibly more than one love, one career?** Like the Internet, where people explore different "personas," give yourself the courtesy of opening your possibilities beyond your present situation. You've got a book inside you that is waiting to come out. Explore the chapters of your timeline and let the journey continue.

4. **Have you ever gone to therapy?** If we don't blink an eye when we take our cars or gadgets in for repair, why is there such stigma when we want to "repair" our psyche? Talking with trusted family members or with professionals, such as counselors, therapists, psychiatrists, and religious leaders, is just as important

to our emotional maintenance. You can always swallow a drug. Talk it out first.

5. **Do you believe you have the power to take charge of your life?** The power of ruling your own emotional planet by not worrying about others' preconceived notions about you is a major takeaway of this book. People are put in your path to test you. If you don't know it yet, many of those who don't have your best interests at heart are jealous. Many will work hard at robbing you of the power to run your life. Don't let them! By living in someone else's vision, you lose out on the joy of living; however, learning through someone else's torment is a lesson worth understanding.

Your life is like a rocket. Lift off and visualize yourself high above it all. Target your mark, and hit your stride. Get to where you need to go by transitioning from the passenger of your life to the pilot of your lifetime. Be the Command Pilot that calls the shots. Others don't rule your planet, you do. What's great for you isn't necessarily perfect for others; however, that's OK. Run your own show the way you want...leave the assholes down on Earth, will you? You have nothing to lose but opportunity.

Endtroduction:

Do it Now!

Before you close the book, I'm back with a final thought that I really wasn't planning on expounding upon, until I looked up at the calendar and noticed that at the time of this writing, it was the twelfth anniversary of my mom Elayne's death. As I reflect upon that moment (which feels like only yesterday), I realize that the experience of losing a loved one—no matter who it is—was another impetus for me to write this book and the inspiration I want you to embrace. We're going to use the idea of a permanent ending as a way to redefine what the phrase "Do it now!" means for you.

On the day Elayne died, she called me in the afternoon at work, something she rarely did unless there was epic family news— like when the cat, Gabriel, died; when Tony and his tanker entered the Persian Gulf; when a stranger like James McBride told her life story on national radio; or in celebration, when Barbra Streisand surprisingly rented the house across the street from her! True story.

The afternoon of her death wasn't ordinary. In fact, it was odd, because she began giving me important life lessons as if she was a female Deepak with a self-help laundry list of "here's what you need to know before I say goodbye." As much as I loved talking with my mom, (and I'm sure from this book you could tell she played an important role in my life), this particular convo could have waited until I got home from work. As she was preaching her words of wisdom, I politely cut her off and said, "Ma, I hear ya; but I gotta go. I'll call you tonight."

The phone call I received less than three hours later was from Tony, telling me Elayne had just passed away.

What?!

Tony was as dumbfounded as I was. It seems as if she just took a nap, had a heart attack in her sleep, and never woke up. Yes, her call during the day came from out of the blue—like her death. The fear of my mom dying was way out of my sights because she didn't have a long bout with cancer or other diseases that prepare families for the big moment. All of my friends and relatives told me how lucky I was that my mom didn't suffer—which is a huge blessing; however, I'm not sure if an abrupt death was easier for those of us still living.

**#Grab the moment now—
tomorrow might not be an option.**

I am sharing this with you because you never know when your last day (or anyone else's) is going to come, and therefore, doing what you want *now* is inevitable, don't you think? If you're a Millennial, chances are you might not have experienced death yet—and that's the rite of youth, I'd say. For anyone who has lost someone you care for, or heard of the death of someone that you didn't know but the news struck a chord, I'm sure you agree that when people die it's unfathomable to picture them as only a memory. Like the beer bottle visual I've mentioned over the course of this book, death is another vision I'd like you to hold onto. You could think of it as a period at the end of the sentence, or you could use it to carry the torch inside you as you thrust your dreams forward.

When Tony went home after Elayne's funeral, the NPR station my mom loved to listen to was permeating throughout the house—he hadn't turned the radio on. As Tony also told me, there was a huge shadow of a dove that opened and closed its wings in flight above where a portrait of him and my mom was displayed. When I went back to my apartment, that same shadow of the ghost-like dove flew inside—as if saying, "I've left, but I haven't left you in spirit."

#Seize the opportunity to take flight.

Since then, the dove has come and gone on two other momentous occasions for me. Once when I fell asleep at the wheel while driving on the Long Island Expressway, the dove woke me up and turned the wheel away from the cement median, avoiding a crash. In Costa Rica on my fiftieth birthday, I was swept away in a riptide. (What an ass I was.) After the third undercurrent and no chance for me to see the water's surface (or so I thought), the dove appeared and darted underwater, pushing me back to the beach as if I was a tiny pebble of sand. My friends, Tim and Rob, didn't have a clue where I was in the water, and seemed totally surprised with how I miraculously showed up, back on shore.

After my mom's passing, and with these signs of the dove surrounding me, I decided to seize the spirit and come to terms that my life's dress rehearsal was over. Now with curtain up, the show is big and bold—not perfect—but very passionate. The dove is inside me and a voice is constantly whispering, "Go ahead, give it a shot—give it a try—go out there and make it all happen. Do it now." No more moments of empty chatter. No more disbelief that what mom and Tony, what friends, and what acquaintances applauded me for was untrue. It *was* true, all of it, and it was time I owned up to the life I was put on the planet to live.

You may not see doves. However, you will see your own version of a bright light of support—if you open your mind to the universe and take in all that you have been given to learn, create and prosper while visiting our planet. Do you want to miss a major opportunity in life before your time is up? C'mon now, be honest with yourself. After reading this book, I hope you're screaming, "Hell, no!" I want you to open the window at night, when the dark sky allows you to see the constellations buzzing. Take in the opportunity, like the stars move in space. This is a moment for you to ask your version of the dove to give you everything you want. This is the opportunity for you to finally throw your skepticism away, and understand that stopping to think and breathe deeply, inhaling and exhaling, and visualizing the success that surrounds you isn't filler for a bad b-roll TV script. It is your life now, and *it is worth living*. What will your tombstone read after you sat around like a pig in shit and did nothing for decades but take, take, take?

**#They were a bunch of procrastinators
who lived life as if they pressed "pause."**

#She was more scared of failing than winning.

It's easy to pin a button on your lapel saying, "Today is the first day of the rest of your life." But when you lose someone you were literally in the middle of a conversation with, the idea of living in the now takes on a whole new meaning.

You can't afford to waste another day of "okay, okays," where your laziness, nervousness, or fear hijacks your life. After all, the mind plays tricks: unless you get up and out and dive into the journey, you realize three months go by—then it's a year's worth of excuses. And your only redeeming factor is that, perhaps, you're still focusing on a dream. Is it a dream or is it a buffer you really don't believe in, simply to shut everyone else up? (After all, no one will fault you if you're "working" on a project.) The truth is that everything that stands in your way is a roadblock to the pot of emotional gold. Remember, time ticks and it is not your friend.... Only you can choose to savor every second, or continue to complain and ultimately give up.

Electronics don't matter. The smartphone isn't going to heaven with you. (Actually, it's going to hell.) You can't take the video games, the Facebook posts, or the nasty Tweets in a goodie bag of good-byes. Emailing, emailing, and more emailing are empty calories. You can't shove all the Louis Vuitton bags, the fancy cars, and the McMansions into your casket—it is all just a bunch of stuff. Sadly, Saks Fifth Avenue is not in Purgatory. What matters are the moments that move your life forward in some way—learning, laughing, helping, confronting, listening, and giving back. Whatever it is, your *life, not your baggage,* is there to drive you through time.

Talk to Me!"

In closing, I hope this book has given you the inspiration (and permission, if you need it) to take your life seriously, make the move to get over yourself and turn on the light of your greatness. Remember Becca's story? Imagine if she really knew deep down inside that she wasn't a piece of shit. No matter what her critical, bitter parents said, she *was* the bread-winner of her family and she had the upper hand on her life, not the other way around.

#This is where you tell your story to me.

Now it's time to spill the beans.

Don't worry if you are being judged, open your heart, and let go of all that stops you in your tracks. Ask for advice if need be. Everyone needs a tune-up, everyone needs to be heard; you are no different. Your stories are worthy of being told, and your dreams and aspirations are worth coming true. You know that somewhere deep down inside of you is a spirit that won't apologize: you were put on this Earth to do extraordinary things. Even if you haven't let that voice within you come out just yet, get started.

If you haven't seen your dove yet, I will volunteer to fly around your shoulder.

#Get out of your own way.

Here's to your fabulous ride of life. Bravo, dear readers. I know you're ready.

Drop me an email at justemailjustin@gmail.com...

...and tell me where or if you've made that 180-degree change in your life, if you're ready to make your dream come true, if you're ready to put the electronics down and make something happen. I wanna help you.

Your heart beats. Your blood flows. Your brain thinks. Your body breathes.

Connect them with purpose.

Acknowledgments

It took me more than ten years to conceptualize and then write this book, and I am so grateful to have this opportunity to share my life, and hopefully help others with the inspiration injected in my story and "steps." Either directly or indirectly, I could not have created this book without the following:

Thanks to the Mango Media mavens for allowing me to step out and dream big! I want to thank my Mango Media publisher, Chris McKenney, and my SVP, Sales & Marketing (and friend), Michelle Lewy, along with the ultra-fab editor Hugo Villabona (the man who pulled one chapter out of my book proposal, thought I had something there, and asked me to make a book concept out of it). To my editor, Brenda Knight (a rare find, a queen of emotional support, and a literary star in her own right) for having the patience to allow me to find my voice. Thanks to Roberto Nunez, my book jacket designer, and to Joshua Bugay and Hannah Jorstad, Sales and Marketing Coordinator. Thank you to Henryk Jaronowski, my copy editor, for taking all of those fucking commas and blah, blah, blahs out of my writing! (And a lot more, trust me.)

Thank you to Mysia Haight, aka Mysia Lee and Mysia Haight-Hoogsteden, my great personal editor and longtime friend who helped me to get out of my own "grammar" way. Mysia is one of those quiet giants who is ready to step out from backstage and write her own book some day. You go, girl!

Thank you to photographer, videographer, and website designer, Charlie Pappas, and Nick Pappas for taking my author photo, designing my book website and filming my digital promos. They could not do their thing without the hardworking woman who keeps their family together: Rebekah Pappas. To little Matty, my best friend!

To some great family members who have passed: My grandmother, Sadie, and grandfather Jacob Loeber, who really knew the definition of work ethic; and my grandmother Mae and grandfather Abe Atlas (the man who gave me my singing voice), who understood how to survive, create and thrive. To my cousin, the late Elliot Taffet, a young boy who died way before he could see his greatness. To the Greek side of my family: Irene Papadopoulos, a woman with a stupendous work ethic (and who makes the greatest spinach pies this side of Greece), and other cousins, including dear Mata, Roula, and Ridi. They love to cook, eat and feed! And they still love calling me "Larry" (with a Greek accent!)

To my late biological father, Robert Louis Loeber, who I think tried his best to be a good dad in the early years—I'll get back to you on that—but lived the last moments of his life in torment.

To June Siegel (my dad Tony's dear soulmate) a true matriarch, and the whole Siegel clan (Jeffrey, Sandra, Richard, Caroline, Hy and Marissa, Jessica and Josh, Caroline and Or, Louis and Rachel, Rebecca, Sarah and Kurt Peters; Brooke, Noah, Spencer, Jordyn, Livia, Dean, Emilia, and Phyllis and Michael, just to name a few, because they have a big family), for warmly accepting me into their respective homes. June and all of her children throw great family functions, I'd say; and everyone in June's family are so super-nice. It all starts at the top!

Only children (like everyone, I'm sure) have a special place in their hearts for their pets (OK, so I'm not sure if I'm going to write another book, so please indulge me!): Salty (the Schnauzer), Frankie (the Sheepdog), Mozetta (the bird), Gabriel (the cat), Lester (the Scottie), and little Rufus (the Silver Dappled Dachshund, who is twelve going on seven!), born on the day of my mom's funeral.

I would not have had a major opportunity, career shift, and life change without the help of Sharyn Rosenblum, who is America's greatest publicist. She and her longtime love, Dereck Walton, are magical people. Sharyn works at HarperCollins, and if anyone reading this book is going to be published by Harper, you'll be in great hands if you work with Ms. Rosenblum. A huge and heartfelt thanks goes to Jacqueline Deval, who is America's greatest publisher, and the author of two books: *Reckless Appetites* and *Publicize Your Book!* Jackie really has been a great support to me over these years, and with her encouragement, has helped me to reach my best potential in publishing.

Thank you to all the other publishing giants who gave me a chance and allowed me to act out (you heard me!), and dream big under their supervision: Bill Shinker, founder of Broadway Books, along with Trigg Robinson, Maggie Richards, Jennifer Swihart Voegele, and Kathleen Spinelli; Buz Teacher, co-creator of Running Press Book Publishers (a true mentor) and his wife, Janet Teacher; and former RP coworkers and friends Brian

Perrin, Bill Lucky, Jennifer Worick, Carlo DeVito and John Whalen. To Jane Friedman, Lisa Herling, Michael Morrison, and Susan Weinberg of HarperCollins; Dan Halpern and Carrie Kania, of Ecco/HarperCollins, along with HC people: Steven Sorrentino, Richard Rhorer, Shelby Meizlik, David Brown, Jane Beirn, Michael McKenzie, Jennifer Robinson, Alberto Rojas, Pam Pfeifer, Tara Brown (my only child girlfriend who shares my birthday with me and with Rupert Murdoch. To Carolyn Reidy of Simon and Schuster, and Judith Curr at Atria Books—these are two ladies who were a great support to me during my mom's passing. To Judith Regan, the last publisher I worked under, who in a very dramatic and indirect way, gave me the courage to start my own business.

Thank you to dear Inger Forland, for instilling your trust in me and giving my boutique business the start it needed; to Jan and Mike Strode of CEO Advisors, who always give me a dose of support, no matter what I do, and Charlie Nurnberg, the creator of Imagine! (Charlesbridge) and Moondance Press (Quarto) who hired us for years and years. To Peter Yarrow and Noel Paul Stookey of Peter, Paul and Mary—they keep hiring us for their numerous important projects (even if they're friends with PR legend, Ken Sunshine!). To Cousin Brucie Morrow—America's greatest radio personality with a heart of gold! To Reeves Lehmann and Annie Flocco of School of Visual Arts whom I love working with year-after-year. To Kris Carr and Brian Fassett: two of the most creative, caring and forward thinking people I know. (Kris changed my life, and thousands of others with her brand, KrisCarr.com and is a true inspiration to the world of wellness.) And to Con Coughlin, an amazing reporter, client, and overall good bloke, along with his wife, "Mrs. C!" Thanks to Georgina Levitt and Roger Cooper for instilling your trust in me. Thank you to SiriusXM's Serena Kodila Regan, Tim Johnson and Megan Kunstra for helping my clients see their dreams; and to SiriusXM's Taylor Strecker her manager, Matthew Toffler, producer Katie Castellano, and associate producer Adam Varano for being generous with me, and my clients.

To my accountant Frank Fabio, along with Phyllis Carlin and Corrine Fabio. Thanks for always being a great support—even during my annual meltdowns! To attorneys Michele Fredman and Joan Feinstein, who helped me to formulate my business. To Ami Wellman, Esq., and to Gabriel Bedoya, and Aisling Curley of the Corcoran Group—who feed my "real estate persona," always have my back, even when I come up with these crazy renovations. To my renovation teams: Tony Savas of S+T Construction, and to Darcy Juliani and the whole team at Juliani's Painting and Contracting.

Thank you to all my employees throughout the years who have made Mouth: Public Relations, and now mouth : digital + public relations successful; most notably, Taiwo Whetstone, Khuong Phan, Patrick Paris, Nadine Hachicho, Sandra Florent, Stephen Francy, and Cydnie Lunsford—all of whom challenge themselves every day and do their absolute best to help me service our clients.

A sincere thanks to ALL my clients who have hired my company. (I'm afraid that if I mention some names and forget others, it will appear as if I haven't appreciated that y'all instilled your trust in me and Mouth.) I appreciate your support—more than you know!! You can find a lot of them— past and present—on my company's website, MouthDigitalPR. com. Thank you to all the literary agents whom I have worked with along the years both for your clients and when I pitch mine to you.

A big hug to everyone in the media (and those who have left the business to reinvent). Since 1993, these people have heard all my pitches, and allowed my company to prosper because they continue to listen to my spiel and book my roster of clients.

Thank you to the JBC Network, Jewish Book Council, and Mitch Kaplan and his team of the Miami Book Fair, for giving me a chance to inspire people in front of audiences around the country.

Thank you to all those who believed in me as a recording artist: To Gary Numan, and his parents, Tony and Beryl Webb for allowing me to step into a big spotlight. To Chris Staines, my English music producer who always had my back and allowed me to dream big. To Charlie Grappone of Vinylmania Records, who helped launch my dance music career in the States; to the late Sergio Munzabai from M + M Productions for the spectacular remixes; to Curtis Urbina of Quark and Emergency Records: How cool was it to be on the same label as Shannon's "Let the Music Play!"; to the Latin Dance Music Superstar, Cyre, who recorded her sexiness on my record.

Thank you to a great group of dear friends who are the brothers and sisters I never had and who make the world a great and fun place to live: Joanie O'Neill, Bob France and John Madera,

Kerry and Steve Bartosik, Bronna and Shelly Lipton, Seda and Arminae Azarian, Scott Fless, Tim Walls, Tim Moir, Rob Taglieri, Paul Olsewski, Tom Bachmann, Rhoda Dunn, Kaylee Davis, Mandi Davis, Joy DiBenedetto, an amazing woman who founded the news organization, HUM NEWS; Faith Childs (of FaithChildsLiteraryAgency.com, who gave me a break by opening up her office to me with welcoming arms, and who is my office mate since 2007), and her husband, Harris Schrank, an expert in fine prints. To Sharlene Martin (what an extraordinary eye for book- to-television projects!) To legendary radio personality, Alice Stockton-Rossini ("that voice, Alice!"), Stacy Schneider, "America's greatest litigator," and Robi Ludwig, PhD—the epitome of thoughtful and kind. To my bestie, Anne ("Annie") Forland and her kind husband, the late Hans Forland, AND the whole Forland and King "mishpucha," (including the late Tom King, "a great builder," Pat, Tomas; Kris, Camille, Ciara, Hans, Caleb, Harry, Aunia; Maisie, Liam; and Frankie...and the list goes on because they have a huge family), for inviting me into their homes as if I was one of their peeps.

And finally, this book is dedicated to two people:

To my stepdad, and real dad, Captain Anthony "Tony" George Papadopoulos, who has always been an inspiration and rock of support to me throughout these years. Tony is the best father anyone on the face of this planet could ask for. He will do anything for anyone and has a heart like no other. Even though I come from a small family, Tony filled the void with his love and care, even after the passing of my mom. Tony's life—from Greece to America—and throughout it all, as the captain of ships—is a passionate and awe-inspiring story you'd want to read about.

And finally, to my mother, Elayne Atlas Loeber Papadopoulos, whom I should have stayed on the phone with the day she died unexpectedly. I really fucked that one up because I was so self-involved the moment she called. Elayne was a mom that all my friends loved because she listened, she took notice, and she cared about everyone, stayed up on the news and wanted to lend support to those who needed it. She was an entrepreneur twice over: a creator of a doll, and an owner of a travel agency—not afraid to shift a gear here and there, and reinvent herself with class and moxie. My mom rarely put herself first—but her presence was enormous and inspiring as she made everyone else around her feel special. My only regret at this juncture, is that you, the reader, did not have the opportunity to have met her.

About Justin Loeber

Veteran publicist Justin Loeber founded mouth : digital +
public relations, www.mouthdigitalpr.com, (formerly known
as Mouth Public Relations), in 2006—boasting more than 550
clients since its inception. The agency is proud to represent
personalities, companies and organizations across the
spectrum—from celebrity, consumer, book, health/wellness,
food, business, new media, beauty/lifestyle and fashion
categories to more than 23 *New York Times* best-selling
authors. Some of the agency's list of clients (both past and
present) include Carly Simon, Kenny Loggins, Kenny Loggins'
Blue Sky Riders, and Kenny Logins' company Higher Vision,
Neil Sedaka and Marc Sedaka, Sally Kellerman, Snooki, Peter,
Paul and Mary, Judy Collins, "Cousin Brucie" Morrow, and the
late "Young and the Restless" star Jeanne Cooper. For three
years, Mouth was proud to be the PR Agency of Record for The

Elf on the Shelf brand (*The Elf on the Shelf* book was a #1 *Wall Street Journal* and #2 *USA Today* best-seller), their animated television feature based on their book, entitled "An Elf's Story," (which aired on CBS and was #1 for children's viewers in their timeslot), as well as their Elf on the Shelf balloon which debuted in the 2012 Macy's Thanksgiving Day Parade. Other notable clients include International and *New York Times* Best-Seller Rick Yancey (*The 5th Wave*), Mitch Albom's 10th Anniversary *New York Times* best-selling edition of *Tuesdays with Morrie*, eco lifestyle expert Danny Seo, and Halo Purely for Pets, America's premier Holistic Pet Care company.

The agency is also proud to have launched *New York Times* best-selling author, filmmaker, Internet star, inspiring cancer survivor and wellness expert Kris Carr and four of her books, including *Crazy Sexy Kitchen*, which debuted at #4 on the *New York Times* Best-Seller list (Advice/How-To) and *Crazy Sexy Diet*, debuted at #6. Other clients include "Operation Respect," a 501(c) 3 organization headed by music icon and activist Peter Yarrow; Ramy Cosmetics; internationally-renowned sculptors Mimi Sammis, and Marie-Helene of Gryphon Fabricators; Lisa Bloom, Esq., Vikki Ziegler, Esq., Kendall Coffey, Esq., Stacy Schneider Esq., and legendary attorney, Raoul Felder; Kripalu, Center for Yoga and Health, International recording artist and healer, Wah!; Ellen Weber Libby, Ph.D., Robin Sol Lieberman, and Rythmia Life Advancement Center (Costa Rica), Ashley Koff, R.D., Michelle Dudash, R.D., Manuel Villacorta, R.D., Simon Sinek, Jack Andraka, Jenn Sincero, Michael Smerconish, Steven Schussler, Jane Velez-Mitchell, Zoe Torres, TV Psychic Matchmaker, Deborah Graham, Marcella Rosen, School of

Visual Arts (SVA) Dusty Film & Animation Festival, Moscow Ballet's Great Russian Nutcracker, adult film star, SEKA; "The Bachelorette" Desiree Hartsock, City Lights Youth Theatre, SAVE (Suicide Awareness Voices of Education), Ground Zero Museum Workshop, Second Chance Toys, Kenny Mayne, Robin Arzon, Jim Leyritz, Linda Cohn, Kenny Mayne and Richard Digger Phelps. Justin also represented Congresswoman Diana DeGette, Ken Blackwell and Ken Klukowski, White House Gate Crashers, Diane Dimond, Howard Clark, Rabbi Shmuley Boteach, Mary Jo Buttafuoco, Tom Sturges, Lucinda Bassett, Geri Spieler, Victoria Bruce, Michaele and Tareq Salahi, Dr. Neal Barnard, Dr. Michael Stone, and Dr. Vijay Vad, Dr. Peter Abaci and his Bay Area Health and Wellness Center, and Dr. Alphonse Tribuiani's Deep Cover Nail System. Mouth also repped MTV's Lisa Ramos, and Dr. Julissa Hernandez. The company worked on campaigns with its clients for milk life, Sabra Hummus, Kind Snacks, Sunkist Fresh Citrus, Symbiotics, New Chapter, and youthH2o, and Pichuberry, Inc.

Mouth was also PR Agency of Record for Globe Pequot Press, Running Press, Cider Mill Press, HCI Books, GMC Publications, Ammonite Press, Button Books, Imagine! Books/Charlesbridge Publishing, Mango Media, PQ Blackwell's Milk Tailor-Made Books, Apollo Publishers, and the party game, Drunk Stoned or Stupid, and The Voting Game. Under the guise of Jan Strode's CEO Advisors, Mouth handled PR outreach for DNA Diagnostic Center (DDC), Ricardo Beverly Hills luggage, and Yevo, amongst others. **For more information about mouth : digital + public relations, please visit www. mouthdigitalpr.com.**

Prior to founding mouth, Justin has held many corporate
executive and managerial roles, including Senior Vice
President, Executive Marketing and Publicity Director
for Regan, which was an imprint of HarperCollins (News
Corporation). He is a former Vice President, Director of
Publicity for Atria, an imprint of Simon and Schuster (Viacom);
Publicity Director for Ecco (HarperCollins); and Director of
Publicity for Running Press Book Publishers. Loeber was one
of the first publicists hired at Broadway Books (Bertelsmann),
was a publicist at William Morrow (Hearst), and started his
publishing career at Villard (Random House).

Over the course of his career, Loeber has restructured
four publicity departments, managed groups of up to 35
employees, and was responsible for publicity and marketing
budgets exceeding $1M. He has created nationally recognized
campaigns in practically every subject area—for celebrities,
fashion icons, sports stars, designers, novelists, doctors,
lawyers, animal lovers, non-profit organizations, restaurateurs,
a presidential candidate, and even one prime minister. Loeber
has spearheaded publicity campaigns for Michael Jordan,
Lawrence Taylor, Cindy Crawford, Olympia Dukakis, Tommy
Lee, Pamela Anderson, Anthony Bourdain, Ewan McGregor,
Tom Perkins, Gloria Allred, Frank Warren, Reverend Bernice
King (Martin Luther King Jr.'s daughter), Kevin Liles
(Executive Vice President, Warner Music Group), Marlo
Thomas, Wanda Sykes, movie producer Lynda Obst, David
Margolick, LeRoy Neiman, Blair Underwood, Jon Gruden,
Leon Uris, Diane McKinney-Whetstone, Jack Newfield,
Lawrence Schiller, Tony Brown, Celia Cruz, Bill Blass, Dr.

Andrew Weil, Lloyd Boston, Dr. Dean Edell, Peter Singer (father of the modern-day Animal Rights Movement), The Telegraph's Con Coughlin, Defense Editor and Aron Ralston (the young Colorado-mountain climber whose story was depicted in "127 Hours," starring James Franco).

Loeber was also instrumental in brokering two book deals at publishing houses he worked for: John Leguizamo's Pimps, Hos, Playa Hatas and All the Rest of My Hollywood Friends (Ecco); and for Patrik Henry Bass and Karen Pugh's, In Our Own Image: Treasured African-American Traditions, Journeys & Icon (Running Press Book Publishers). On the first anniversary of 9/11, Loeber was the only publicist at ground zero in Shanksville, PA, where he represented New York Times reporter Jere Longman and his book, Among the Heroes. He also managed national publicity for Singapore's Senior Prime Minister Lee Kuan Yew, and orchestrated a publicity tour for Colombian presidential candidate Ingrid Betancourt whose book, Until Death Do Us Part, exposed the tragic underground affiliation between her country's government and its drug cartels.

In the 1980s he was a solo pop recording artist in the United Kingdom, (performing his own "Shivers Up My Spine" and "Vibrations of the Night" for Numa Records); where he was discovered by and toured with English music legend Gary Numan. Soon thereafter, Loeber inked three more recording contracts in the States (Vinylmania Records, Emergency Records, and Sid Bernstein's The New York Music Company). Two more twelve-inch dance music records—"Those Words" (Vinylmania); and "Love Me or Leave Me" (Emergency) were

Loeber's original, published dance and techno-pop records heard around the world without Loeber ever seeing any royalties beyond advances paid to him.

For more than a decade, as a hobby, Loeber buys, renovates, designs and sells homes in Manhattan, Brooklyn, Hamptons, Connecticut, Philadelphia and Woodstock, New York–one of which was featured in the *New York Times* Real Estate section. Justin lives between New York City and Weston, CT. *Get Out of Your Own Way Guide to Life: 10 Steps to Shift Gears, Dream Big, Do it Now!* (Mango Publishing) is Loeber's first book.

For more information about the book, please visit www.getoutofyourownwaybook.com

CPSIA information can be obtained
at www.ICGtesting.com
Printed in the USA
BVOW08s1906101117
500037BV00001B/1/P